Speak Japanese!

すぐに使える日本語会話
超ミニフレーズ 発展210 中〜上級編

210 Additional Super-Miniature Phrases
for Immediate Use
in Japanese Conversation
"Intermediate to Advanced Level"

監修
水谷信子
Mizutani Nobuko

高橋尚子／松本知恵／黒岩しづ可
Takahashi Naoko　Matsumoto Chie　Kuroiwa Shizuka

Jリサーチ出版

はじめに Foreword

　だいぶ日本語が使えるようになったと思えるけど、もっとうまくなりたい、言いたいことをぴったりした表現で言えるようになりたい——そう感じている人は実は多いのではないかと思います。そういう人の気持ちに添いたい、意欲に応えたいと思うわたしたちの願いから、この「日本語会話超ミニフレーズ」のシリーズが生まれました。

　このシリーズでは「ごちそうさまです」「お疲れさまです」のような、いわゆる日常生活の決まり文句にとどまらず、皆さんが自分の考えや気持ちを的確に伝えて、日本人とのコミュニケーションを生き生きと効果的に行うために役立つフレーズを紹介します。

　例えば、何か頼む場合、ただ「お願いします」と言う代わりに「お手数をおかけします」「勝手を言ってすみません」と言ったほうがまじめな態度が相手に通じますし、頼まれても断らなければならないとき、「だめです」と言うより「難しいです」と遠回しに答えることもできるといいと思います。

　また、相手が結論を急ぎすぎる場合、ただ「待って」と言うより「しばらく様子をみましょう」と言ったほうが信頼を得ることになるでしょう。何かを評価するとき、「いいですね」だけでなく「気に入った」「申し分ない」と言えばもっと積極的な気持ちが表せます。

　相手の冗談をうけて「よく言うよ」「またー。冗談ばっかり」と返すことができれば、相手の距離がぐっと近くなるでしょう。

　前作では、初級学習者でもむりなく覚えられるようなやさしいフレーズを取り上げましたが、今回はそれを発展させ、会話の内容をさらに広げ、深めてくれるようなフレーズを集めました。たとえば「うんざりする」「納得いかない」「そんなもんだよ」「カチンと来る」のような、日本人が本音をもらすときのさりげない表現も入れました。こうした表現も理解できるようになれば、もっと日本語で会話をする楽しさが増すでしょう。

　皆さんが日本語でのコミュニケーションの中で、受け身にならず、伸び伸びと自分を表現していってくださることを望んでいます。そのためにこの本がお役に立てば幸いです。

水谷信子

Do you ever feel as though your Japanese has reached the point where you are able to use it well, but you still want to become better and able to find just the right phrase? We think there are many people in that situation, and this Japanese Conversation Super-Miniture Phrases series was born from our wish to help those people fulfill their desires.

This series includes more than just stock phrases you use in daily conversation such as "go-chisousama desu" and "otsukaresama desu." In these pages, we introduce useful phrases that will allow you to more precisely express your thoughts and feelings in lively, effective conversations with Japanese people.

For example, if someone helps you, a simple "onegaishimasu" does allow you to ask for things, but your seriousness will come across better if you were to say "otesuu o okakeshimasu" or "katte o itte sumimasen." When you have to turn down a request, it is also better to reply with the more roundabout "muzukashii desu" instead of "dame desu."

Also, when someone rushes too quickly to a conclusion, it will be easier to gain their trust by using "shibaraku yousu o mimashou" rather than a simple "matte." When evaluating something, your feelings will be asserted more strongly by using "ki ni itta" or "moushibun nai" instead of a plain "ii desu ne." And if you're able to reply to someone's joke with "yoku iu yo" or "mataa. Joudan bakkari," you'll surely find yourself closer to them in no time at all.

The previous title introduced simple phrases that even beginners could remember without much trouble. This title expands on those, broadening the kinds of conversations considered to gather a deeper collection of phrases. For example, there are subtle expressions used by Japanese people when they reveal their true feelings, such as "unzari suru," "nattoku ikanai," "sonna mon dayo," and "kachin to kuru." Speaking in Japanese will become even more enjoyable once you are able to understand these kinds of expressions.

We hope that all of you will become able to communicate in Japanese as not passive receivers, but as free and active participants able to express their own thoughts, and we truly hope that this book can help you achieve that goal.

目次 Table of Contents

はじめに　Preface ･････････････････････････････････ 2
学習の流れ　How to proceed with your studies ･････････ 10
この本の使い方　How to use this book ･･･････････････ 12
CDの使い方　How to use the CD ･････････････････････ 14

すぐに使える 日本語会話超ミニフレーズ　発展210
210 Additional Super-Miniature Phrases for Immediate Use in Japanese Conversation

あ／A

1　あきれる　I'm dumbfounded ･････････････････････ 16
2　焦った　I got flustered ･･････････････････････････ 17
3　当たり前です　Of course; nothing unusual ･････････ 18
4　あっという間　It was over in the blink of an eye ･････ 19
5　あと一歩　Just a step away ･････････････････････ 20
6　あやしい　That sounds fishy ･････････････････････ 21
7　あり得ない　Out of the question ･･････････････････ 22
8　あわてなくていい　You don't have to rush ････････････ 23
9　いい加減だなあ　You're Irresponsible ･････････････ 24
10　いい加減にして　Cut it out ･････････････････････ 25
11　いい線いってる　You're on a right track ･･････････ 26
12　いいな　I envy you ･･･････････････････････････ 27
13　言いにくいんですが　It is hard to say, but ････････ 28
14　言い訳はいい　No need for an excuse ･･････････ 29
15　言えてる　You can say that again ･･････････････ 30
16　意外　Surprisingly; hard to believe ･･････････････ 31
17　一応　At any rate; for now ･････････････････････ 32
18　一か八か　Sink or swim ･･･････････････････････ 33
19　言ってくれればよかったのに　You should've told me ････ 34
20　いつでも言ってください　Tell me whenever ････････ 35
21　いつものこと　This is normal; usual (thing) ････････ 36
22　今一つ　Lacking; not totally ････････････････････ 37
23　意味がわからない　I don't understand (what you mean) ････ 38
24　いやだ　I don't want to ････････････････････････ 39
25　イライラする　Ticked off ･･･････････････････････ 40
26　うっかりしてた　I was being careless ･･････････････ 41
27　うまく言えない　It's hard to explain ･･･････････････ 42
28　うまくいってる　Going well ････････････････････ 43
29　うんざり　Boring ･････････････････････････････ 44
30　偉い　Great ････････････････････････････････ 45

#	日本語	英語	ページ
31	お言葉に甘えて	If it's all right; accept (your) kind offer	46
32	お先に	Ahead of you	47
33	おしゃれですね	How stylish	48
34	落ち込む	Down; depressed	49
35	おっしゃるとおりです	Exactly as you say	50
36	追ってご連絡します	I will contact you later	51
37	お手数をおかけします	Sorry for the trouble	52
38	思ったとおり	Just as I thought	53
39	恩に着る	Indebted to	54

か／K

#	日本語	英語	ページ
40	カチンと来る	Pissed off	55
41	がっくり	Bummed out	56
42	かっこ悪い	Uncool	57
43	勝手にやれば？	Why don't you do it yourself?	58
44	勝手を言ってすみません	I'm sorry for my selfish request	59
45	変わらないです	The same (as always); hasn't changed	60
46	考えられない	Unthinkable	61
47	関係ない	It doesn't matter	62
48	感心する	I'm impressed	63
49	勘弁して（ほしい）	Give me a break	64
50	聞いてない	I never heard about that	65
51	気が重い	Feel down; feel depressed	66
52	気が利くね	How thoughtful	67
53	気が気じゃなかった	Was on pins and needles	68
54	気が進まない	Not in the mood	69
55	聞かなかったことにして	Pretend you didn't hear that	70
56	気が向いたら（でいい）	You can if you feel interested	71
57	期待してたんだけど	I had my hopes up	72
58	きついです	It's rough; tight	73
59	気に入った	～ love it; ～ like it	74
60	気に触ったらごめんなさい	Sorry if I rubbed you the wrong way	75
61	気になる	Bothers me	76
62	気のせい	(Your / my) imagination	77
63	決まってる	Of course	78
64	気持ちいい	Feel so good	79
65	気持ち悪い	Feel sick; feel bad	80
66	急な話で恐縮ですが	I apologize for suddenly bringing this up	81
67	急に言われても困る	You can't suddenly say that	82

5

目次

68	今日はここまでにしましょう	Let's stop here for today	83
69	気楽に	Take it easy	84
70	きりがない	There's no end to it	85
71	具合はどう？	How do you feel?	86
72	くよくよしないで	Don't fret over	87
73	検討します	Let me think it over	88
74	誤解です	You're mistaken	89
75	ここだけの話ですが	Just between you and me	90
76	言葉も出ない	Nothing to say	91
77	子どもじゃないんだから	You're not a child	92
78	ご迷惑じゃないですか	Am I bothering you	93
79	これでいい？	Is this okay?	94
80	こんなチャンスはめったにない	There aren't many chances like this	95
81	こんなもんじゃない？	Isn't that (about) what you'd expect? ; Is it any surprise?	96

さ／S

82	最高	It's amazing; It's the best	97
83	最低	The worst	98
84	さっぱりわからない	I don't have a clue	99
85	至急、お願いします	Please do it as soon as possible	100
86	失礼だなあ	How rude	101
87	死ぬほど	To death; It almost killed me	102
88	しばらく様子を見ましょう	Let's wait and see	103
89	冗談じゃない	You're joking	104
90	知らない	You're on your own; not my problem	105
91	素晴らしい	Wonderful	106
92	ずるい	Not fair	107
93	鋭いなあ	How sharp	108
94	全然	(Not) at all	109
95	そういうわけにはいかない	I can't let that happen	110
96	そう思わない？	Don't you think so?	111
97	そこをなんとか	Can't you (please) make it work	112
98	そっか	Is that so	113
99	それじゃ	Well then	114
100	それでか	So that's why	115
101	それどころじゃない	This isn't the time for that	116
102	それなりに	In its own way; accordingly; as it is	117
103	それは痛い	That hurts; that's awful; It's painfu	118

Table of Contents

104	それはそうだ	Of course	119
105	それはそうと	Anyway; putting that aside	120
106	それはないよ	No way; unreasonable	121
107	それはよかった	I'm glad it worked out	122
108	それほどでもないです	Not really; It's nothing	123
109	それを聞いて安心した	I'm relieved to hear that	124
110	そんな感じです	Something like that	125
111	そんなに（あんまり）急かさないで	Don't rush me so much	126
112	そんなばかな	Such nonsense; How can that be?	127
113	そんなはずはない	It can't be so	128
114	そんな日もあるよ	There are days like that	129
115	そんなもんだよ	That's how it is	130

た／T

116	大したことない	It's nothing special; It's no big deal	131
117	大したもんだ	Impressive; a big deal	132
118	耐えられない	Can't bear	133
119	だから言ったのに	That's what I said	134
120	だよね	I knew it; I thought so	135
121	頼りにしてます	Counting on you	136
122	違う	No; That's wrong	137
123	力が出ない	Have no strength	138
124	調子はどう？	How are you doing?; How is it coming along?	139
125	冷たいなあ	You're cold	140
126	つらい	Tough; difficult	141
127	同感です	I agree	142
128	同情するよ	I sympathize	143
129	どうってことない	No big deal	144
130	どうでもいい	Don't care a bit	145
131	どうなってる？	What's going on?	146
132	どうやって？	How?	147
133	道理で	That makes sense	148
134	特にない／特には	Not really; nothing in particular	149
135	特に問題ない	There's no particular problem	150
136	どっちもどっちだ	Neither is better than the other	151
137	取り返しがつかない	There's no taking that back	152

な／N

138	なかなか	Not bad; I'm impressed	153
139	泣きたくなる	It makes me want to cry	154

7

目次

140	情けない	Pitiful	155
141	納得いかない	Hard to accept	156
142	何？	What is it?	157
143	何が言いたいの？	What are you trying to say?	158
144	何もなければいいけど	I hope nothing happens	159
145	何やってるの？	What are you doing?	160
146	何よ／何だよ	Seriously?; What is it?	161
147	何を考えているんですか	What are you thinking?	162
148	悩む	I can't choose; I can't decide	163
149	なんかあったの？	Did something happen?	164
150	なんだかなあ	I don't get it	165
151	何て言ったらいいか	What should I say	166
152	何てことだ	I can't believe it	167
153	何でもない	It's nothing	168
154	何とも言えない	There's nothing I can say	169

は／H

155	ばかばかしい	Absurd; pointless	170
156	ばかみたい	That seems ridiculous	171
157	恥ずかしい	I'm ashamed; It's embarrassing	172
158	はっきりして	Be more clear	173
159	初耳です	The first I've heard of it	174
160	話が違う	Not what I've heard	175
161	ひどくない？	Isn't it awful?	176
162	他人事じゃない	This isn't someone else's problem	177
163	一言多い	(To) say too much	178
164	凹む	Feel depressed	179
165	別に怒ってない	It's not like I'm mad	180
166	勉強になる	It's instructive	181
167	ぼちぼち	Getting better; not too bad	182
168	ほっとく	Leave ～ alone	183
169	ほっとしました	I'm relieved	184
170	ほどほどにね	Take it easy	185
171	本気で言ってるの？	Are you serious?	186

ま／M

172	任せた	I'm leaving it to you	187
173	またー	Oh you; again?	188
174	また頑張ろう	Let's try again another time	189
175	またにしよう	Let's do it another time	190

8

Table of Contents

176	まだまだこれからです	(It's) only getting started	191
177	間違ってたらごめんなさい	I'm sorry if I'm mistaken	192
178	まったく	For Christ's sake; come on	193
179	まねできない	No one else can do it; I can't do it	194
180	見損なった	Misjudged; lost respect	195
181	みっともない	Not a pleasant sight	196
182	見てられない	I can't bear to look	197
183	見直した	Changed my opinion	198
184	難しいです	It's difficult; not easy	199
185	無責任だなあ	How irresponsible	200
186	無茶です	That's impossible	201
187	無理しなくていい	You don't need to force yourself	202
188	迷惑です	What a nuisance; feel annoyed	203
189	めんどくさい	It's tiring; It's too much work	204
190	もう限界	I'm at my limit	205
191	申し分ない	It's perfect	206
192	もうだめだ	Can't keep going	207
193	もっともです	I agree	208
194	物足りない	Lacking; insufficient	209

や／Y

195	やった	(I / We) did it	210
196	やっと一段落する	Finally able to take a breath	211
197	やめとく	I'll hold off	212
198	やるしかない	Have to do it	213
199	やるね	Nice job	214
200	やればできる	You can do it if you try	215
201	許せない	Unforgivable	216
202	よくあること	That happens often	217
203	よく言うよ	You're one to talk; Are you kidding?	218
204	読めない	Hard to read	219
205	余裕がある	Can afford to	220
206	余裕がない	Can't afford to	221

わ／W

207	わかる	I know; I understand	222
208	わざとらしい	Sounds fake or insincere	223
209	悪いね（感謝の気持ち）	Sorry; my bad (meaning thanks)	224
210	悪かった（謝罪の気持ち）	Sorry; my bad (meaning an apology)	225

さくいん（英語）　Index (English) · · · · · · · · · · · · · · · · · · 226

学習の流れ　How to Proceed with Your Studies

この本では、次のステップで学習します。しっかり練習を続けることで、"日本語会話の基礎力"が自然に身につきます。

STEP 1 ▶▶▶ フレーズの意味を理解する

まずフレーズの意味、フレーズが使われる場面、フレーズの意図や効果を押さえます。

STEP 2 ▶▶▶ 会話例を聞く

会話例を聞きます。会話が行われている場面や話し手の気持ちを想像しながら、フレーズの意図や効果を確かめながら聞きましょう。また、特に短いフレーズについては、音のアクセントやイントネーションに注意しましょう。

STEP 3 ▶▶▶ フレーズを言う

耳慣らしの練習に続いて、今度は CD の音声のすぐ後を追いかけるように、まねして自分で言ってみましょう。それに慣れてきたら、本を見ないで音だけで練習をしましょう。

STEP 4 ▶▶▶ くりかえし練習

くりかえし学習することで、どんどん効果が増します。CD の音を気軽に聞き流すだけでもいいですし、声に出して練習すると、さらにいいでしょう。☞「CD の使い方」(p.14)

In this book, proceed with your studies according to the steps listed below. By practicing consistently and thoroughly, you will naturally achieve an ability in the basics of Japanese conversation.

STEP 1 ▶▶▶ Understand the meaning of the phrase

First, get an understanding on the meaning of the phrase, image where the conversations are taking place, and understand the intention of the phrase and its effectiveness.

STEP 2 ▶▶▶ Listen to the conversation examples

Listen to the conversation examples. Imagine where the conversations are taking place, and the speakers feelings, while ascertaining the intention of the phrase and its effectiveness. Additionally, be careful of accents and intonations especially for short phrases.

STEP 3 ▶▶▶ Say the phrases out loud

After the listening practice, try to mimic the sounds of the CD directly after they are spoken. Furthermore when you become familiar with the phrase, practice the same way by only listening to the sounds without looking at the textbook.

STEP 4 ▶▶▶ Repeat Exercises

You will become proficient through repetition drills. You can simply listen to the CD, but it would be best to practice the drills out loud. (See: How to Use the CD, p.14)

この本の使い方　How to use this book

● テーマとなるフレーズ
「です・ます」体と「だ・である」体、両方の場合があります。
※ 会話例での形は、必ずしも このままではありません。

● フレーズの訳
英語でこれに相当するフレーズや意味の近い表現を挙げています。

● さくらのマーク
基本的な意味や働きを示しています。

● ポイント
使用場面や話し手の気持ちなど、意味の理解や使い方のポイントを示しています。

● 会話例を紹介しています。

● 会話の場面などの補足情報を加えています。

---

10 いい加減にして
Iikagen ni shite

Cut it out; That's enough

☆ Indicates feeling bothered because someone's words or actions have gone too far.

POINT
▶ Used in cases of severe anger or strong disapproval.
▶ It is also used in imperative forms such as "Iikagen ni shinasai." or "Iikagen ni shiro."

❶ No kidding
A：さっきからふざけたことばかり言って。もう、いい加減にして！
B：ごめん、ごめん。

A: You've been doing nothing but kidding around. That's enough, already!
B: Sorry.

❷ No money
A：ごめん、ちょっとお金貸してくれない？
B：もう！ 私はＡＴＭじゃないんだから！いい加減にして！

A: Hey, could you lend me a little money?
B: Really, I'm not an ATM! Cut it out!

❸ Dependence
A：ほんと、困りました。どうしたらいいですか。
B：知りませんよ。甘えるのもいい加減にしてください！

A: I'm really in a bind. What should I do?
B: It's not my problem. Quit depending on me for everything!

Variations

❹ Order from a customer
A：また内容変更してきたよ。
B：また!? もう、いい加減にしてほしいなあ。

A: They've changed the details of their order again.
B: Again? I wish they'd get it straight already.

25

● 応用・発展的な会話例を紹介しています。動詞を活用したものや他の文型と結びついたもの、また、意味の似た語など関連表現を取り上げています。

● フレーズは五十音順に並んでいます。該当する行（あ行、か行…）を濃くしています。

12

● **Phrases in this Book**

Phrases introduced in this book are in both "*desu / masu*" and "*da / de aru*" form. They do not necessarily have to be used in the exact form they are introduced in through the sample conversations.

● **Translations of Phrases**

Phrases are also translated into English phrases with similar meanings or uses.

● **Sakura Symbol**

The basic meaning and function of phrases is printed next to a sakura symbol.

● **POINT**

POINTs are also provided that further explain the meaning and usage of phrases. For example, they may describe situations and emotions that call for a phrase's use.

● Examples of a phrase's use in conversation are given on each page.

● These usage examples also include supplemental information, such as where or why the conversation is taking place.

---

10 いい加減にして

Iikagen ni shite

Cut it out; That's enough

✿ Indicates feeling bothered because someone's words or actions have gone too far.

POINT
➡ Used in cases of severe anger or strong disapproval.
➡ It is also used in imperative forms such as "*iikagen ni shinasai*." or "*iikagen ni shiro*."

❶ **No kidding**
A: さっきからふざけたことばかり言って。もう！ いい加減にして！
B: ごめん、ごめん。

A: You've been doing nothing but kidding around. That's enough, already!
B: Sorry.

❷ **No money**
A: ごめん、ちょっとお金貸してくれない？
B: もう！ 私はＡＴＭじゃないんだから！ いい加減にして！

A: Hey, could you lend me a little money?
B: Really, I'm not an ATM! Cut it out!

❸ **Dependence**
A: ほんと、困りました。どうしたらいいですか。
B: 知りませんよ。甘えるのもいい加減にしてください！

A: I'm really in a bind. What should I do?
B: It's not my problem. Quit depending on me for everything!

Variations

❹ **Order from a customer**
A: また内容を変更してきたよ。
B: また!? もう、いい加減にしてほしいなあ。

A: They've changed the details of their order again.
B: Again? I wish they'd get it straight already.

25

● Example conversations are meant to be practical and constructive. These introduce verbs used, connections with other sentence patterns, and related expressions with terms that have similar meanings.

● Phrases are arranged according to the Japanese syllabary. The corresponding column (*a*, *ka*, etc.) is in bold.

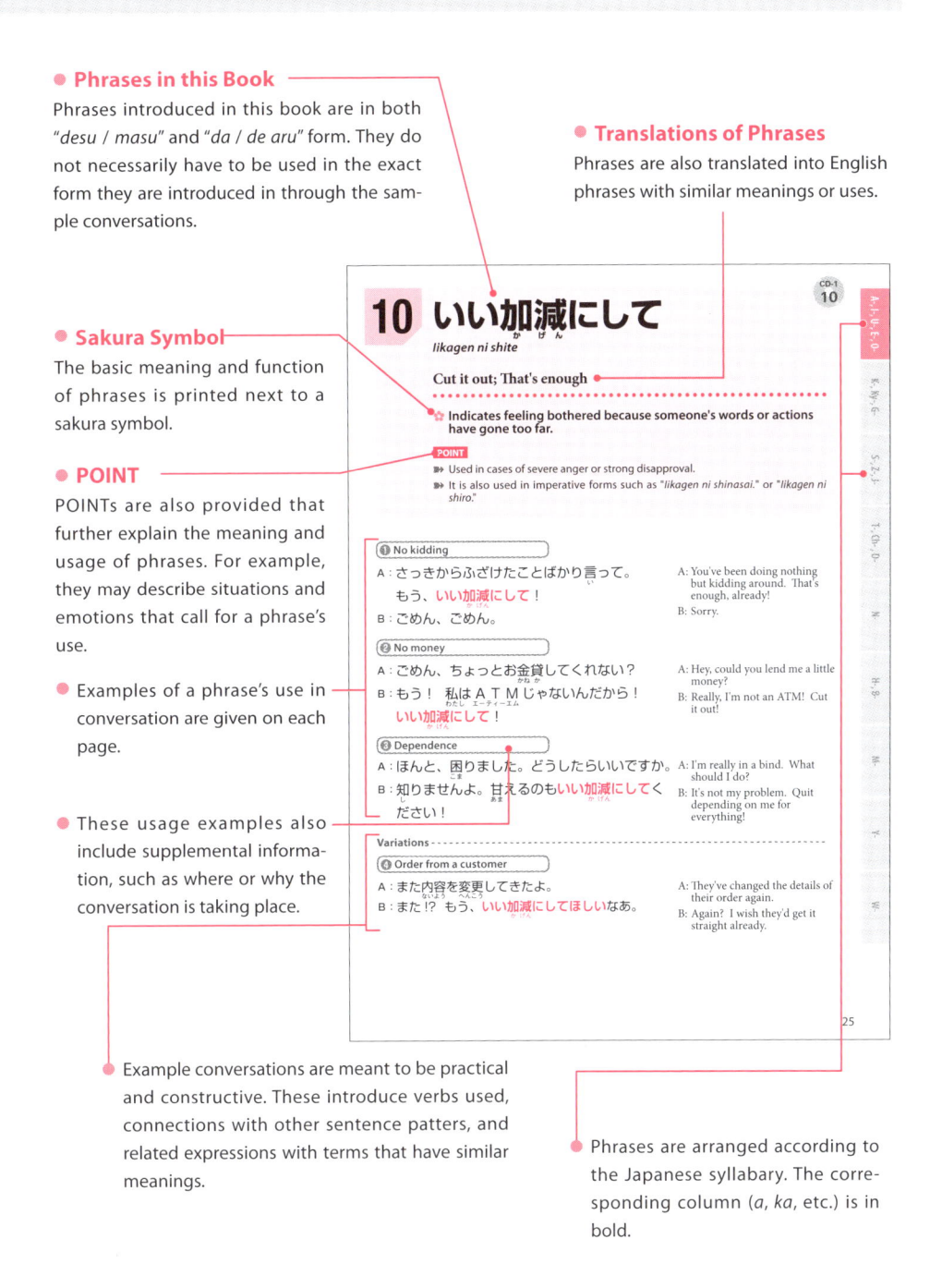

CDの使い方

付属CDには、会話例の会話文（日本語）がすべて収録されています。

❶ まず最初に、1ページの中で紹介されている会話例の文をすべて読みましょう。一つ一つ意味を理解し、会話が行われている場面をイメージしてみましょう。

❷ 次に、本を見ながらCDを聞きましょう。どんな音で話されているか、イントネーションなど、音のニュアンスをつかみながら確認しましょう。

❸ 本を見ながらCDの音を聴き、すぐ後を追いかけるように、まねして口に出しましょう。

❹ 今度は本を見ないで、同じように練習しましょう。

How to Use the CD

The enclosed CD contains all of the conversation examples of the conversation texts in Japanese.

❶ First, read all of the conversation examples listed on the first page. Try to understand the meaning of each, and imagine where the conversations are taking place.

❷ Next, listen to the CD while you follow the text. Pay close attention to the sounds of the speech, and nuances of the sound, such as accents and intonations.

❸ Listen to the CD while following the text. Try to mimic the sounds aloud directly after they are spoken.

❹ Now practice the same way again without looking at the textbook.

すぐに使える
超ミニフレーズ
発展210

**210 Additional Super-Miniature Phrases
for Immediate Use in Japanese Conversation**

1 あきれる *Akireru*

I'm dumbfounded; I'm scandalized; I'm disgusted

✿ It is used to express the feeling of being astounded and dumbfounded, as to someone's selfishness or senseless speech and behavior.

POINT

➡ This word includes the delicate shade of meaning that one is disgusted, or disapproving.

❶ About a colleague

A: 森さん、また遅刻だって。
B: また？ ほんと、**あきれる**なあ。

A: Mori-san is late again?
B: Is he really? I feel utterly scandalized.

❷ After the Festival

A: すごいゴミだね。
B: うん。マナーが悪い人が多いんだね。**あきれる**よ。

A: That's a lot of trash.
B: Yeah. Which means, there are so many people without manners. I'm disgusted.

❸ About a boss

A: なんであんなことで怒るんだろう。
B: まったくね。いつものことだけど、**あきれる**よ。

A: Why is he so worked up about something like that?
B: Absolutely. As is often the case with him, and I'm fed up.

❹ When in a group tour

A: **あきれた**よ。彼、また一人でどっか行っちゃったよ。
B: また!? 困った人だね。

A: I'm amazed that he has gone somewhere again alone.
B: Not again!? He's really a pain in the butt.

❺ Blame someone

A: もっと説明してくれればよかったのに。
B: また人のせいにするの!? **あきれる**なあ。

A: I wish you had explained to me more in detail.
B: You're blaming others again!? You're hopeless.

2 焦った Asetta

I got flustered

✿ Expresses feelings of surprise or confusion when something unexpected happens.

POINT
➡ "*Aseru*" is used when irritated because something must be done quickly, while "*asetta*" is used after things have calmed down.

---

❶ After shopping

A：さっきレジで財布忘れたことに気づいて**焦った**よ。
B：私もたまにやる。**焦る**よね

A: I just thought I forgot my grocery bags and I got flustered.
B: I do that sometimes too. It really does make you flustered.

❷ At a test site

A：やっと来た。遅いから心配したよ。
B：寝坊しちゃって。ほんと、**焦った**。

A: You're finally here. You were late so I was worried.
B: I overslept. I was really flustered.

❸ A small child

A：朝起きたら子供がいなくて**焦った**よ。
B：え！ 大丈夫だったの？
A：うん。ベッドの下にいた。

A: When I woke up in the morning, my child was gone and I was flustered.
B: What! Was she okay?
A: Yes, she was under the bed.

❹ Inside a train

A：よかったね、電車、間に合って。
B：うん。**焦った**よ、もう。

A: It's a good thing we made it onto this train.
B: Yes, I was getting flustered.

17

3 当たり前です *Atarimae desu*

Of course; obviously; nothing unusual

❖ This means "anybody would do the same" or "it's common sense to be like that."

POINT
➡ This is almost the same meaning as "*Toozen desu*." but is more emphatic and is more often used in conversation.

❶ For a beginner

A：ミスしてばかりで、すみません。
B：まだ新人なんだから、当たり前だよ。

A: I am making lots of mistakes. Sorry.
B: You are still a beginner. That's nothing unusual.

❷ Looking at a parking fee

A：えっ、有料なの？
B：当たり前だよ。ただのわけないじゃない。

A: What? Do we have to pay?
B: Of course. It's not free, you know.

❸ Hearing words of thanks

A：本当に助かりました。ありがとうございます。
B：このぐらいは当たり前ですよ。

A: It was really helpful. Thank you very much.
B: I didn't do anything unusual.

❹ A new house

A：当たり前だけど、きれいな家ですね。
B：ずっとこうだといいんですが。

A: It's clearly a lovely house.
B: I hope it will always be like this.

❺ Urban life

A：車を持っているのは当たり前ですか。
B：いや、都会ではそうでもないですよ。

A: Do people usually own a car?
B: No, not so much in urban areas.

4 あっという間 *Attoiuma*

It was over in the blink of an eye

❁ It is used to express the feeling that time went by in an instant.

POINT
▶▶ It is often used when talking about the past in a retrospective glance.

---

❶ 5th Year in Japan

A：日本に来て、もう５年になるんですか。
B：ええ。**あっという間**でした。

A: Is it already your fifth year in Japan?
B: Yes. It went by like a flash.

❷ At the end of the year.

A：もう 12 月かあ。
B：今年も**あっという間**だったね。

A: Oh, it's already December.
B: This year has come to an end before we knew it.

❸ The next day

A：昨日は楽しかったね。
B：うん。**あっという間**に時間が過ぎたよ。

A: We really had fun yesterday.
B: Yeah. It ended all too soon.

❹ At the end of the summer vacation

A：もう夏休みが終わるね。
B：ほんと、**あっという間**だった。

A: Summer vacation is ending soon.
B: Yes it is. It went by in an instant.

❺ Before dinner

A：おいしそう！ 手間がかかったでしょう。
B：ううん。意外に簡単で、**あっという間**にできるの。

A: It looks delicious! I'm sure it took a great deal of time to make all this.
B: No, not at all. It's surprisingly easy, and it doesn't require much time.

19

5 あと一歩 Ato ippo
いっぽ

Just a step away

✿ **Used to express a situation where only a little more was needed to accomplish a goal or target.**

POINT
- "*Ato ippo desu*" is used to encourage someone when they are close to achieving their goal.
- "*Ato ippo datta ne*" is used to console someone who was unable to achieve their goal.
- "*Ato ippo datta noni*" is used by someone who was unable to reach their goal to describe their own situation.

❶ Test preparation

A: もう疲れたよ。勉強したくない。
B: 合格まであと一歩なんだから、がんばって！

A: I'm tired. I don't want to study.
B: You're just a step away from passing, so keep at it!

❷ Watching a sports match

A: もうちょっとで勝てたのになあ。
B: うん。あと一歩だったね。

A: We were so close to winning.
B: Yes, we were just a step away.

❸ Choosing a theme

A: レポートのテーマは決まりましたか。
B: いえ、あと一歩というところです。

A: Did you decide on a report theme?
B: No, I'm just a step away from it.

❹ Completion in sight

A: 完成まであと一歩というところで問題が起きたんです。
B: え？ どんな問題ですか。

A: A problem occurred when we were just a step away from finishing.
B: Hm? What was the problem?

❺ After vote totals are announced

A: あと一歩及ばず、落選してしまいました。
B: 応援していたんですが、残念です。

A: I was unable to take that last step and lost the election.
B: I was supporting you, but that's too bad.

6 あやしい *Ayashii*

That sounds fishy

❀ **It is used to express the feeling of doubt toward someone's speech and behavior, or toward a thing or situation.**

POINT
➡ It is used when you cannot believe what someone said, or when you feel that the other person is hiding something from you.
➡ It is even used concerning yourself, when you are not sure about the fact.

---

① At the book store

A：この本を読むだけで幸せになるんだって。
B：何、それ。絶対にあやしいよ。

A: You will have good fortune just by reading this book.
B: What's that. That is really fishy.

② About a colleague

A：あの二人、最近あやしいと思わない？
B：うん。付き合ってるかもね。

A: Don't you think those two are having some kind of affairs recently?
B: I've noticed it too. Maybe they're going out.

③ Not overlooking

A：今、何を隠したの!? あやしいなあ。
B：なんでもないよ。

A: What did you hide right now? You're suspicious.
B: It's nothing of your concern.

④ Saying things doubtfully

A：うーん、たぶん6時には行けると思うんだけど…。
B：ほんとに？ あやしいなあ。

A: Hmmm. I think I'll be able to come by 6 o'clock.
B: Are you sure? I doubt you can.

⑤ Time Limit

A：この作業、4時に終わるかなあ？
B：4時はちょっとあやしいかも。でも、4時半までには終わると思う。

A: Do you think this project will end by 4 o'clock?
B: 4 o'clock is doubtful, but I'm sure we can finish it by 4:30.

7 あり得ない *Arienai*

Out of the question

❋ Used to indicate that there is zero possibility of something occurring.

POINT

➡ A strong denial of the possibility that something could ever happen as being unthinkable.

---

❶ Harsh heat

A：なに、この暑さ！
B：ほんと。あり得ないよ。

A: What's with this heat?
B: I know. It's out of the question.

❷ A meeting

A：ごめん、ごめん。
B：1時間も遅刻するなんてあり得ない！

A: Sorry, sorry.
B: Being an hour late is out of the question!

❸ Under consideration for marriage?

A：彼はどう？ 結婚相手として。
B：えー、あり得ないよ。

A: What about him as a potential husband?
B: What? That's out of the question.

❹ Chances of winning

A：ワールドカップで日本が優勝する可能性ってある？
B：それはあり得ないよ。

A: Is there any chance that Japan could win the World Cup?
B: It's out of the question.

❺ Goals that are too high

A：売上目標はいくらだって？
B：1000万円。そんなの、あり得ないよね。

A: What were our sales goals again?
B: 10 million yen. That's out of the question, wouldn't you say?

8 あわてなくていい *Awatenakute ii*

You don't have to rush

❋ It is an expression used to let someone know that there is no necessity of rushing.

POINT
➡ It is often used to calm someone down, or when in a situation where rushing could lead to failure.

---

❶ Before leaving

A：もう出ないと間に合わないんじゃない？
B：**あわてなくていい**よ。10分くらい余裕あるから。

A: I don't think we'll make it in time if we don't leave now.
B: No need to rush. We have a margin of 10min.

❷ To the new hire

A：なかなか仕事が覚えられなくて…。
B：**あわてなくていい**よ。ゆっくり覚えれば。

A: It's taking me time to learn this job...
B: You don't have to rush. You can take time learning.

❸ Before leaving

A：ちょっと待って。すぐに終わらせるから。
B：そんなに**あわてなくていい**よ。急いでないから。

A: Wait a second. I'll finish it up real quick.
B: You don't have to rush so much. I'm not in a hurry.

Variations -

❹ At a bus stop

A：もう、バス、全然来ない。
B：**あわてなくていい**よ。

A: The bus isn't arriving at all.
B: No need to rush.

23

9 いい加減だなあ *Ikagen da naa*

You're irresponsible

🌸 It is used to express the feeling of disapproval, to someone who has an irresponsible attitude or who scamps work.

POINT

➡️ It includes the feeling that the work should be done in a proper way, without cutting corners.

❶ Mail order

A：「明日には発送します」って昨日言ってたのに、在庫がないって。
B：何、それ？ **いい加減だなあ**。

A: They said, "We'll send it to you tomorrow", but now they're saying that they don't have any stocks.
B: What's that? They're really irresponsible.

❷ At the work place

A：いいよ、そんな感じで。誰もそんなに見ないから。
B：えー、**いい加減だなあ**。

A: That's good enough. No one looks at it carefully enough anyway.
B: Wow, you really do a sloppy job.

❸ Time for bus arrival

A：とりあえずバス停まで行こうよ。ちょっと待てば来るよ。
B：**いい加減だなあ**。時間くらい調べて行こうよ。

A: Let's start off with going to the bus stop. The bus should arrive while we wait there for a few minutes.
B: That's irresponsible. Let's go after checking the time table.

❹ Seasoning a dish

A：塩入れたかなあ。…まあ、いいや。薄かったら後で入れれば。
B：なんだか**いい加減だなあ**。

A: Did I add salt in it? Uhm. Well, I would season it later if I feel short of taste.
B: Isn't it a little sloppy?

10 いい加減にして
Iikagen ni shite

Cut it out; that's enough

✿ **Indicates feeling bothered because someone's words or actions have gone too far.**

POINT
- Used in cases of severe anger or strong disapproval.
- It is also used in imperative forms such as "*Iikagen ni shinasai.*" or "*Iikagen ni shiro.*"

❶ No kidding

A：さっきからふざけたことばかり言って。もう、**いい加減にして**！
B：ごめん、ごめん。

A: You've been doing nothing but kidding around. That's enough, already!
B: Sorry.

❷ No money

A：ごめん、ちょっとお金貸してくれない？
B：もう！　私はＡＴＭじゃないんだから！**いい加減にして**！

A: Hey, could you lend me a little money?
B: Really, I'm not an ATM! Cut it out!

❸ Dependence

A：ほんと、困りました。どうしたらいいですか。
B：知りませんよ。甘えるのも**いい加減にしてください**！

A: I'm really in a bind. What should I do?
B: It's not my problem. Quit depending on me for everything!

Variations

❹ Order from a customer

A：また内容を変更してきたよ。
B：また!?　もう、**いい加減にしてほしい**なあ。

A: They've changed the details of their order again.
B: Again? I wish they'd get it straight already.

25

11 いい線いってる *Ii sen itteru*

You're on a right track; It's in line

❀ It is an expression used to affirmatively evaluate the situation of a matter, acknowledging that it is at a pretty high level.

POINT
➡ When it is used in answering to some question or a supposition, it means that it is "close to the correct answer."

---

❶ While going through a business proposal

A：この企画、どうでしょうか。
B：**いい線いってる**と思うよ。

A: What do you think of this project?
B: It's in line with what I think.

❷ At the pastry shop making a trial piece

A：どうですか。
B：うん、**いい線いってる**。これならお店でも出せそう。

A: What do you think of it?
B: I think you're on a right track. Maybe with this you can start your own shop.

❸ New face scouting audition

A：この人はどうですか。
B：彼もなかなか**いい線いってる**んだけど、何か足りないんだよなあ。

A: What do you think of this person?
B: He's quite close to the person we're looking for, but he's lacking something.

❹ Newly bought second-hand motor bicycle

A：中古だったら15万円くらいですか。
B：**いい線いってる**ね。14万円だよ。

A: If this is a second-handed motor bike, is the price about 150,000 yen?
B: You were close. It is 140,000 yen.

12 いいな *Ii na*

I envy you

✿ It is used to express your envious feeling toward someone's situation.

POINT
➡ The polite way of using this word is "*ii desu ne.*"

---

❶ Plan for the holidays

A：年末は家族でハワイに行くんです。
B：へー。**いいな**。

A: I'm going to Hawaii with my family during the year-end holidays.
B: Wow. I envy you.

❷ Incentive

A：今回はボーナスがちょっと多かった。
B：**いいな**。うちは出なかったよ。

A: The bonus I received this time was a bit more than last time.
B: I envy you. We had none.

❸ Children Circumstances

A：子どもは**いいな**。何も悩まなくていいから。
B：子どもにも子どもの悩みがあるんだよ。

A: I envy children. They have no worries at all.
B: Even children have their own worries.

❹ Location of a house

A：みんな、**いいな**、家が近くて。
B：そうか。田中さんは結構遠かったもんね。

A: I envy all of you. You guys live so close.
B: I know how you feel Tanaka-san. You come from a distance.

13 言いにくいんですが *Iinikui n desu ga*

It is hard to say

🌸 It is an expression used as an introduction, when saying things that may not be acceptable to others, or when giving unfavorable opinion on someone.

POINT
➡ It is used when warning others, saying things against others' expectation, criticizing someone, or requesting personal wishes.

❶ Overlapping

A：**言いにくいんですが**、実はその日仕事が入って…。
B：えっ、来られないの？ 残念。

A: It is hard to say, but to tell you the truth I have work that day.
B: Oh! You cannot come? That's unfortunate.

❷ Disliking certain types of people

A：**言いにくいんだけど**、実は石原さんが苦手で…。
B：それで今日の食事会、行かないんだ。

A: It is hard for me to say this, but to tell you the truth I don't like Ishihara-san so much.
B: That's why you're not coming to the dinner party tonight?

❸ About the hair style

A：ちょっと**言いにくいんだけど**、絶対、前の髪型のほうがいいと思う。
B：やっぱりそうか…。

A: It's hard to say, but I'm sure your former hair style was better.
B: I know it.

❹ An honest opinion

A：ちょっと**言いにくいんですが**、原さんのさっきの話…。
B：ちょっと変だよね。私もそう思った。

A: It is hard to say, but the thing Hara-san just said…
B: Doesn't make sense. I think so too.

14 言い訳はいい *Iiwake wa ii*

No need for an excuse

🌸 **It is used to express one's feeling of not wanting to, or has no intention of listening to an excuse concerning the mistake which the other person made.**

POINT
- It is used to express one's feeling, that the other person should humbly accept the blame.
- It is said when the other person starts making excuses.

---

❶ Arriving late

A：バスが全然来なくて…。
B：**言い訳はいい**よ。

A: The bus took forever to come...
B: Don't make excuses.

❷ On the phone

A：いろいろ急ぎの件が続いて、うっかり送るのを忘れてしまいました。
B：**言い訳はいい**から、早く送ってください。

A: I forgot to send you the stuff, since there were so many things of great urgency.
B: You can come up with the excuses later, but please first send them to me.

❸ Tidying up

A：時間がなくて、なかなか手が付けられないんだよ。
B：**言い訳はいい**から、早く片付けて。

A: I'm not able to start cleaning, as I can't find time to do them.
B: Forget the excuses, and clean up quick.

❹ In a difficult situation

A：確かにぼくが悪かったんだけど、いろいろ重なってたんだよ。
B：**言い訳はいい**から、しっかり反省して。

A: It was certainly my fault, please understand that there were so many things one after another.
B: No excuses. You should really repent.

15 言えてる Ieteru

You can say that again

✿ **An expression used to acknowledge the validity of something another has said.**

POINT
➡ Used to express feelings of agreement that what has been said is exactly right.

---

❶ About a commonly-known individual

A：あの食生活じゃ、体壊して当然だと思うんだよね。
B：**言えてる**！

A: It's no wonder that his health deteriorated when he ate like that.
B: You can say that again!

❷ At work

A：部長のことだから、まだ怒ってそうですね。
B：ああ、**言えてます**ね。

A: It's about the department chief, so he's probably still angry.
B: Yeah, you can say that again.

❸ A proposal

A：それ、二人でやったほうが早くない？
B：**言えてる**ね。そうしよう！

A: Wouldn't it be faster to do that with two people?
B: You can say that again. Let's do that!

❹ A way of looking at things

A：収入が多いからって、貯金ができるわけじゃないと思うんです。
B：確かに、**言えてます**ね。

A: Just because you have a lot of income doesn't mean that you'll be able to save money.
B: Yes, you can say that again.

16 意外 *Igai*

Surprisingly; hard to believe

✿ This indicates surprise when an expectation and actual result are dramatically different.

POINT
➡ When used as an adverb, both "*igai to*" "*igai ni*" are correct.

---

❶ With a friend

A：マイク、ピアノが弾けるんだって！
B：え、意外！

A: Mike told me he can play the piano!
B: Really? Hard to believe!

❷ About clothes

A：意外と似合ってるよ。
B：意外ってどういうこと!?

A: You look surprisingly good in it.
B: Why? What do you mean by "surprisingly"?

❸ First experience

A：意外に難しかったな。
B：簡単そうなのにね。

A: It was unexpectedly difficult.
B: Although it looked easy….

❹ At a friend's wedding

A：いい式だったね。
B：うん。あの気の強い彼女が泣くなんて意外だったな。

A: It was a nice ceremony.
B: Yes. It was a surprise that such a strong-willed woman cried.

❺ Something you dislike

A：意外かもしれないけど、実は犬が苦手なんです。
B：ほんとに!? それは意外。

A: You might be surprised, but I don't like dogs.
B: Really? That is surprising!

17 一応 *Ichioo*
いちおう

At any rate, tentative, for now

❃ (1) Indicates that something is more or less as it should be, although it may not be fully adequate.
(2) Indicates taking some action that seems adequate as at least a tentative measure, but without 100% certainty.

POINT

➡ Used when there is concern about whether something is 100% certain, or there are elements of uncertainty.
➡ Even when something is 100% certain, it may be used jokingly to imply "Even though you don't think so." ⇒ No.6

❶ With a colleague

A：文章のチェック、一応済んだけど、もう一度自分でも見直してね。
B：うん。ありがとう。

A: I gave your paper the once-over, but you should revise it again yourself.
B: OK. Thanks.

❷ About the departure day

A：いつ出発するか、決めた？
B：はい、一応。

A: Have you decided when to depart?
B: Yes, tentatively.

❸ How to use

A：ちゃんとマニュアル読んだ？
B：一応。ま、大丈夫だよ。

A: Have you read the manual properly?
B: More or less. But it'll be OK.

❹ Different than usual

A：今日はスーツなんだ。
B：一応ね。初めて会う人だから。

A: You're wearing a suit today.
B: Yeah, I thought I'd put on a suit at least. It's because I'm meeting someone for the first time.

❺ Confirmation

A：彼女にはメールした？
B：うん。でも、返事がないから一応電話もかけてみる。

A: Did you email her?
B: Yeah. But she didn't reply, so I'll just try phoning her as well.

❻ Age

A：マイケルはまだ未成年でしょ？
B：こう見えても、一応25歳なんですが。

A: Michael, aren't you still underage?
B: I may look young, but in fact I'm 25.

18 一か八か (いちかばちか) *Ichi ka bachi ka*

Sink or swim; all or nothing

❋ Used when entrusting the outcome of an action to fate if you don't know whether it'll succeed or not.

POINT
- Originally used as a gambling term.
- Often used when the chances of success are low, but when the results of a success are great.

❶ Confession

A: 卒業したら会えなくなるし、一か八か告白してみる。
B: 付き合ってくれたらいいね。

A: I won't be able to see her again after graduating, so I'll try confessing to her. It's all or nothing.
B: It'd be nice if she agreed to go out with you.

❷ Seeing an help wanted ad

A: どうしよう。応募してみようかなあ。
B: 一か八か受けてみたら？

A: What should I do? Maybe I should try applying.
B: Why not try? It's all or nothing.

❸ Starting a business

A: 今の仕事をやめて、一か八か会社を作ろうかと考えてます。
B: え？ そうなんですか。

A: I'm thinking of quitting my job and starting my own company, sink or swim.
B: What? Is that right?

❹ Conveying your determination

A: 自信は全然ないけど、一か八か、やってみます。
B: うん。後で後悔しないほうがいいよ。

A: I'm not confident at all about it, but I'll give it a try, sink or swim.
B: Okay. It's better to not have to regret it later.

❺ A request

A: 一応、頼むだけ頼んでみようと思うんです。
B: うん。一か八か、やってみないとわからないからね。

A: I thought I'd at least try making the request and seeing how it goes.
B: Yeah. You won't know unless you try, sink or swim.

19 言ってくればよかったのに

Itte kurereba yokatta noni

You should've told me

❊ Used together with feelings of both regret and dissatisfaction that something did not go as well as it could have because someone did not tell you something.

POINT
➡ While it is sometimes used out of consideration to others, it is also sometimes used out of one's own interests.

❶ Birthday

A：私、昨日が誕生日だったんです。
B：えー！ 言ってくれればよかったのに！

A: My birthday was yesterday.
B: What! You should've told me!

❷ Wanting to take a break

A：ごめん、ちょっと休んでもいい？ 朝から足が痛くて。
B：なんだ、早く言ってくれればよかったのに！

A: Sorry, could we take a little break? My feet have hurt since this morning.
B: What? You should've told me that earlier!

❸ On the phone

A：今日は帰り遅くなるから、晩ご飯いらない。
B：遅いよー。作る前に言ってくれればよかったのに。

A: I'll be coming home late today, so I won't need dinner.
B: You're telling me now? You should've said that before I made this food.

Variations

❹ Something you don't understand

A：そんなことで悩んでたの？ だったら、聞いてくれればよかったのに。
B：そうですね。

A: That's what you were worried about? You should've just told me, in that case.
B: You're right.

❺ Difficult work

A：えっ、一人で全部運んだの？ 言ってくれれば手伝ってあげたのに。
B：すみません。

A: What, you carried all of this yourself? I would've helped you if you told me.
B: I'm sorry.

20 いつでも言ってください

Itsudemo itte kudasai

Tell me whenever

✿ Used to communicate feelings that you are willing to help someone whenever they require.

POINT
▶▶ Includes feelings of telling someone they do not need to be reserved.

---

❶ With a coworker

A：ありがとうございます。助かりました。
B：いえいえ。困ったときは**いつでも言ってください**。

A: Thank you, you really helped me out.
B: Not at all. You can tell me whenever if you're in trouble.

❷ With a friend.

A：困ったときは**いつでも言って**。
B：うん。またお願いするかもしれない。

A: Tell me whenever if you're in trouble.
B: Okay. I may ask you again.

❸ With a coworker

A：手伝いが必要だったら、**いつでも言って**。
B：ありがとうございます。

A: If you need help, tell me whenever.
B: Thank you.

Related phrases

❹「いつでもどうぞ」

A：またお願いしてもいいですか。
B：もちろんです。困ったときは**いつでもどうぞ**。

A: May I ask you for this again?
B: Of course. Whenever you would like to ask me.

35

21 いつものこと *Itsumo no koto*

This is normal; usual (thing)

❀ An expression used to show that there is no need for surprise because while something may normally be unusual, it is regular in a certain situation.

POINT
➡ Often used to speak about people or time periods.

❶ Isn't he cold?

A：えっ？　こんなに寒いのに、ジムさん半袖!?
B：彼、暑がりだから。**いつものこと**だよ。

A: What? It's this cold outside, but Jim-san is wearing short sleeves?
B: He tends to be hot. This is normal for him.

❷ Waiting

A：あれ？　田中さん、まだかな？
B：だろうね。あの人が遅刻するのは**いつものこと**だもの。

A: Huh? Is Tanaka-san still not here?
B: Probably. It's normal for her to be late.

❸ In a car

A：渋滞につかまっちゃいましたね。
B：この時間は**いつものこと**ですよ。

A: Looks like we got hit by traffic.
B: It's normal for this hour.

❹ Because of the weather

A：まだ頭痛いの？　大丈夫？
B：うん、雨の日は**いつものこと**だから。

A: Your head still hurts? Are you okay?
B: Yes, this is normal for me when it rains.

22 今一つ (いまひと) *Ima hitotsu*

Lacking; not totally

❀ Used to express feelings of dissatisfaction because something does not fully live up to what you were originally seeking.

POINT

➡ "*Imaichi* (今一)", which comes from "*ima hitotsu* (今一つ)," is a more informal expression and is broadly used, primarily among younger generations.

❶ Evaluation

A：ねえ、このケーキどう？
B：うーん。味(あじ)はおいしいんだけど、見(み)た目(め)が今(いま)一(ひと)つかな。

A: Hey, how is this cake?
B: Hm. It tastes good, but the presentation is lacking.

❷ A problem

A：無事(ぶじ)に解決(かいけつ)してよかったね！
B：うん。でも、今(いま)一(ひと)つすっきりしないんだよね。

A: It's a good thing we were able to fix it!
B: Yes, but for some reason I'm not completely satisfied.

❸ Doubts

A：質問(しつもん)はありませんか。
B：すみません、このCとDの違(ちが)いが今(いま)一(ひと)つよくわかりません。

A: Do you have any questions?
B: Sorry, I still don't fully understand the difference between C and D here.

❹ Effects

A：薬(くすり)の効(き)き目(め)はどう？
B：うーん。今(いま)一(ひと)つ。

A: Is the medicine effective?
B: Hm. It's lacking.

❺ Ease of use

A：今度(こんど)のスマホ、今(いま)一(ひと)つ使(つか)いにくいんだよな。
B：そのうち慣(な)れるよ。

A: The new smartphone I have is a little hard to use.
B: You'll get used to it sooner or later.

23 意味がわからない *Imi ga wakaranai*

I don't understand (what you mean)

❀ Used to express feelings of doubt or confusion at someone's intentions or the point of something.

POINT
➡ Often used to express feelings of dissatisfaction or irritation, rather than to mean "I don't understand the meaning of these words."

---

❶ About a movie

A：最後のシーンはどういうこと？
B：うーん、ちょっと意味がわかんないね。

A: What happened in the last scene?
B: Hmm, I didn't really understand.

❷ At the workplace

A：部長は急に不機嫌になるから困るよね。
B：ほんと。意味がわかんない。

A: Isn't it hard to deal with the department chief? He'll suddenly get in a bad mood.
B: It really is. I don't understand.

❸ A couple

A：もう何も言わない。好きに決めていいよ。
B：え、なんで？ 意味がわからない。

A: I won't say anything else. You decide on your own.
B: What, why? I don't understand.

❹ A couple

A：昨日のメール、ちょっと意味がわからないんだけど。
B：何でもないよ。無視して。

A: I didn't really understand your email yesterday.
B: It's nothing. Ignore it.

24 いやだ *Iyada*

I don't want to

A straightforward expression of not wanting to do something or wanting to avoid it.

POINT
➡ Written in kanji as "*iya desu*." Has the same negative emotional meaning as "*kirai*" and "*kirau*."

---

❶ Bad at something

A：今度、ちょっとしたパーティーの司会やってくれない？
B：いやだよ。そういうの、苦手だから。

A: Could you head the next little party we have?
B: I don't want to. I'm bad at those kinds of things.

❷ Slow going at work

A：このままじゃ、休日に出ることになるかも。
B：そんなのいやですよ。

A: We might have to come to work on our day off at this rate.
B: I don't want to do that.

❸ At home

A：後で買い物に行く？
B：いやだよ。こんなに雪降ってるのに。

A: Do you want to go shopping later?
B: I don't want to. Not when it's snowing this much.

❹ Dissatisfied with something

A：山田さんから部長に言ってくださいよ。
B：えー、いやですよ。

A: You tell the division chief, Yamada-san.
B: What? I don't want to.

25 イライラする *Iraira suru*

Ticked off

❋ To feel irritated or angry when things do not go as expected or when there is no time.

POINT
➡ Sometimes used when one's poor health leads to frustration or sensitivity.

---

❶ Traffic

A：すごい渋滞だね。
B：もう、**イライラする**。

A: Look at all this traffic..
B: It really ticks me off.

❷ At the bus stop

A：もう、バス、全然来ない。遅れちゃうよ。
B：まあ、そう**イライラしない**で。

A: Oh, the bus isn't coming at all. We'll be late.
B: Now, don't be so ticked off.

❸ Not enough sleep

A：なんか、**イライラしてる**よ。
B：ああ…、昨日寝てないんだよ。ごめん。

A: You seem ticked off for some reason.
B: Oh... I didn't sleep last night. Sorry.

❹ About a coworker

A：彼、ちょっとのんびりしすぎじゃない？
B：うん。彼と話してると、ときどき**イライラする**。

A: Isn't he a little too laid back?
B: Yes. Talking to him sometimes makes me feel ticked off.

26 うっかりしてた *Ukkari shiteta*

I was being careless

❁ **To forget to do something or to make a mistake because of a lack of attentiveness.**

POINT

➠ *"Ukkari"* means "to be absentminded and inattentive as a result," and the adverb version of this, *"ukkari ~suru"* is also frequently used.

❶ At the workplace

A：先方（せんぽう）にメールしてくれた？
B：すみません、**うっかりしてました**。

A: Did you send them an email?
B: Sorry, I was being careless.

❷ Taking something out of the refrigerator

A：あ〜あ、これ、もう期限切れ（きげんぎれ）。
B：**うっかりしてた**。もったいなかったね。

A: Look, this has already expired.
B: I was being careless. What a waste.

❸ Late night

A：ああ、もう終電（しゅうでん）ない。
B：やばい。**うっかりしてた**。

A: Ah, there aren't any trains left tonight.
B: Oh no. I was being careless.

Variations

❹ At the workplace

A：しまった。**うっかり**ファイル消（け）しちゃった！
B：うそ！ それ、大事（だいじ）なデータじゃないの？

A: Now I did it. I carelessly deleted the file!
B: No! Wasn't that an important piece of data?

41

27 うまく言えない *Umaku ienai*

It's hard to explain

✿ Used to express feelings of frustration over something being difficult to put in words.

POINT
➡ "*Umaku ienai kedo, ~*" is placed in front when attempting to explain even when it is difficult to express something in words.

---

❶ Change

A: 彼女、ちょっと変わったと思わない？
B: え？
A: **うまく言えない**けど、なんか優しくなった気がする。

A: Don't you think she's changed a little?
B: What?
A: It's hard to explain, but it feels like she's nicer now.

❷ A farewell when returning to a home country

A: じゃ、元気でね。
B: うん、ありがとう。国に帰れるのはうれしいけど…ああ、**うまく言えない**…。

A: Be well.
B: Yes, thank you. I'm happy that I get to go back to my country, but...oh, it's hard to explain...

❸ Thoughts on a film

A: 昨日の映画、どうだった？
B: うん、よかったよ。**うまく言えない**けど、すごく感動した。

A: How was the movie yesterday?
B: Oh, it was good. It's hard to explain, but I was really moved.

❹ Communicating through a letter

A: 口では**うまく言えない**から、手紙書いてみた。後で読んで。
B: ほんと？　ありがとう。

A: It's hard for me to explain in person, so I tried writing a letter. Read it later.
B: Really? Thank you.

28 うまくいってる *Umaku itteru*

Going well

❖ When things are in a good state or are proceeding in a good state.

POINT
➡ Used about work, activities, plans, relationships with others, and so on.

❶ About work

A：久しぶり。最近、仕事はどうですか。
B：ちょっと忙しいですが、まあ、**うまくいってます**よ。

A: It's been a while. How has your work been lately?
B: It's been a little busy, but it's going well.

❷ Job hunting

A：就職活動は**うまくいってます**か。
B：それが、あんまり…。なかなか面接に受からないんです。

A: Is your job hunt going well?
B: Well, not really… I'm having trouble passing interviews.

❸ Plans

A：そういえば、あの企画はどうなったの？ 進んでる？
B：ええ。特に問題ありません。**うまくいってます**。

A: By the way, how did those plans turn out? Are they proceeding?
B: Yes, there's been no problem. They're going well.

❹ A relationship

A：あの二人、**うまくいってる**のかなあ。
B：さあ、どうでしょう。

A: I wonder if those two are getting along well.
B: Who knows.

29 うんざり *Unzari*

Boring; tiresome

✿ It is a feeling that you don't want it anymore, as things of the same kind are repeated.

POINT
➡ It is used when the kind of situation you hate continues, and one cannot bear it anymore.

❶ Recent weather

A：最近、ずっと雨だね。明日もだって。
B：明日も？ **うんざり**するなあ。

A: Recently, it is raining the whole time, and it is rainy again tomorrow.
B: Tomorrow again? I'm sick and tired of it.

❷ Boss' lecture

A：あー、もう。部長の説教には**うんざり**。
B：ほんと。今日も長かったね。

A: Arh. The manager's lecture is so tiresome.
B: I agree. It was very long again today.

❸ A do-over

A：これ、また一からやり直しだって。
B：また？ もう、**うんざり**。

A: We need to redo this from start again.
B: Again? I'm tired of it.

❹ The same food

A：最近忙しいから、毎日、コンビニのお弁当かパン。
B：私も。でも、さすがに**うんざり**してきたな。

A: Since I'm quite busy recently, I'm just having boxed lunch or bread bought from the convenient store everyday.
B: Me too. However, as is to be expected, I'm feeling tired of it.

30 偉い *Erai*

Great

❋ Used to highly evaluate someone's actions as wonderful and grand, and to express feelings of amazement and praise.

POINT
- Another meaning of *"erai"* is "A high social status or position."
- An evaluative term, which means it is not used for those superior to you.

❶ A new employee
A: 新人の原さん、朝早く来て頑張ってるね。
B: うん。偉い。

A: Hara-san, the new employee, has been coming in early and working hard.
B: Yes. She's great.

❷ An university student
A: 大学の授業料は、全部自分で稼いで払っています。
B: それは偉いですね。大変でしょう。

A: I'm paying my university tuition entirely on my own.
B: That's great. It must be tough.

❸ A small helper
A: 娘は毎日夕食の手伝いをしてくれるんです。
B: まだ小さいのに偉いですね。

A: Our daughter helps us with dinner every night.
B: Even though she's still so young. How great.

❹ Store worker
A: 毎日朝から晩まで働いて、偉いですね。
B: いえいえ。この仕事が好きなんですよ。

A: Working every day from morning to night, that's amazing of you.
B: Not at all. I enjoy this job.

❺ A wonderful proposal
A: これ、ジムさんが提案したんだ。偉い！
B: ちょっと思いついただけです。

A: Jim-san, is this your proposal, right? How great!
B: It was just a little something that came to me.

45

31 お言葉に甘えて　O-kotoba ni amaete

If it's all right; accept (your) kind offer

❀ A set phrase used when accepting someone's kindness and doing as they propose.

POINT
➡ "*Amaeru*" means "to impose on someone's kindness without reservation."

❶ Being driven
A：駅まで車で送りますよ。
B：そうですか。じゃ、**お言葉に甘えて**。

A: I'll drive you to the station.
B: Really? Well, if it's all right with you.

❷ An invitation
A：うち、すぐ近くだから寄っていってください。
B：じゃ、**お言葉に甘えて**。

A: Please come by our home, it's very close.
B: Then I'll accept your kind offer.

❸ At a restaurant
A：今日は私がおごりますよ。
B：そうですか。では、**お言葉に甘えて**。ごちそうさまです。

A: I'll pay for this.
B: Really? Well, if it's all right with you. Thank you for the meal.

❹ At work
A：予定あるんでしょ？ 残りはやっとくよ。
B：そうですか。じゃ、**お言葉に甘えて**。

A: Don't you have plans? I'll take care of the rest.
B: Really? In that case, I'll accept your kind offer.

❺ At a visited home
A：たくさんあるから、好きなだけ持って帰って。
B：では、**お言葉に甘えて**。

A: We have a lot of them, so take as many home as you want.
B: Then I'll accept your kind offer.

32 お先に *O-saki ni*

Ahead of you

❖ **An expression used to casually inform someone that you will be doing something before them.**

POINT
- A polite form of "*saki ni*", "*o-saki ni*" is the normal way of saying the phrase.
- "*O-saki ni doozo.*" is used when you wish to encourage someone to go before you.

❶ At the workplace

A：では、お先に失礼します。
B：お疲れさまでした。

A: Please excuse me first.
B: Good work today.

❷ Before starting a meal

A：冷めちゃうから先に食べて。
B：じゃ、お先に。いただきます。

A: Go ahead and eat first, it'll get cold.
B: Okay, then I'll go ahead and eat.

❸ When getting off an elevator

A：どうぞお先に。
B：あ、すみません。

A: Please go ahead of me.
B: Oh, thank you.

❹ At a restaurant for lunch

A：田中さん、もう会社に戻るんですか。
B：1時から会議なんです。皆さんはゆっくりしていってください。じゃ、お先に。

A: Are you going back to the company already, Tanaka-san?
B: I have a meeting from 1. None of you should rush, though. Please excuse me first.

47

33 おしゃれですね *Oshare desu ne*

How stylish

1: An expression used to praise someone or something's degree of refinement.
2: An expression used to praise the attention someone gives to their clothes, makeup, and so on.

POINT
➡ Used to describe various things other than people, including clothes, furniture, utensils, stores, towns, and so on.

❶ With an acquaintance

A：その帽子、**おしゃれですね**。
B：ほんとですか。昨日買ったんです。

A: That hat is stylish.
B: Really? I bought it yesterday.

❷ While visiting someone's home

A：このキッチン、とても**おしゃれですね**！
B：ありがとうございます。

A: This kitchen is very stylish!
B: Thank you very much.

❸ At a cafe

A：このお店、お気に入りなんだけど、どう？
B：うん、すごく**おしゃれ**！

A: I like this store, what about you?
B: Yes, it's very stylish!

❹ About clothes

A：ローラさんって、いつも**おしゃれですね**。
B：そんなことないですよ。でも、そう言われるとうれしいです。

A: Laura-san, you're always very stylish.
B: That's not true. But I'm happy to hear you say that.

34 落ち込む *Ochikomu*

Down; depressed

❋ The state of being unenergetic and emotionally saddened due to troubles, the shock of a failure, regrets, and so on.

POINT
▶ In particular, this describes a state of having no energy and having a dark expression.

❶ Immediately after buying something

A：そのスマホ、買ったばかりだったの？
B：そう。もう、落ち込むよ。

A: So you just bought that smartphone?
B: That's right. How depressing.

❷ Losing data

A：彼、データ、全部消しちゃったんだって。
B：えっ。それは落ち込むね。

A: I heard he deleted all of his data.
B: What? That'd make you feel down.

❸ Being rejected

A：突然「別れよう」って言われたら、そりゃあ落ち込むよ。
B：そうですね…。

A: Suddenly being told "we should break up" would depressing anyone.
B: You're right...

❹ A failed transaction

A：そんなことがあったんですか。大変でしたね。
B：はい。さすがにその時は落ち込みました。

A: Is that what happened? That sounds tough.
B: Yes. And that did get me down.

49

35 おっしゃるとおりです

Ossharu toori desu

Exactly as you say

❀ Used to express feelings of being satisfied with what someone has said or to affirm their words.

POINT
➡ The form "*ossharu toori ~ desu*" is also used.
➡ Sometimes used in an intentionally sarcastic tone when receiving advice or a sound argument from someone close to you.

❶ On the phone

A：金額が3000円以上になると、送料が無料になるんですか。
B：はい、おっしゃるとおりです。

A: Is shipping free if the amount is over 3,000 yen?
B: Yes, that's exactly right.

❷ At the workplace

A：このやり方は丁寧だけど、時間がかかりすぎるなあ。
B：はい。おっしゃるとおりです。

A: This is a very thorough way of doing things, but it takes too much time.
B: Yes, exactly as you say.

❸ Teacher and student

A：アニメフェアは行きましたか。
B：はい。先生のおっしゃるとおり、すごい人でした。

A: Did you go to the anime fair?
B: Yes. There were so many people there, exactly as you said, sensei.

❹ Advice

A：うまくいかないのは、あなたに才能がないからじゃなくて、努力が足りないからだよ。
B：はいはい、おっしゃるとおりです。

A: It's not going well because you're not trying hard enough, not because you don't have the talent for it.
B: Yeah, yeah. Exactly as you say.

36 追ってご連絡します

Otte go-renraku shimasu

I will contact you later

❁ **To let someone know something later, and not at the current time.**

POINT
➡ Often used to mean "once it is ready" or "closer to the date", but the amounts of time in those situations vary.

❶ Details

A：では、詳しくは追ってご連絡します。
B：わかりました。

A: So I'll contact you later with more details.
B: I understand.

❷ A store for an event

A：忘年会の店、決まった？
B：すみません、まだなんです。決まり次第、追ってご連絡します。

A: Did you decide on the store for the year-end party?
B: Sorry, not yet. I will contact you later once we do.

❸ At an interview

A：今日はこれで終わりです。結果は追ってご連絡します。
B：ありがとうございました。

A: That's it for today. We will contact you later with the results.
B: Thank you very much.

❹ Concrete details

A：じゃ、15日、よろしく。
B：わかった。で、待ち合わせは？
A：ああ、待ち合わせか…。追って連絡するよ。

A: In that case, I'm looking forward to the 15th.
B: Alright. So, where should we meet?
A: Oh, a meeting place... I'll contact you later about that.

37 お手数をおかけします

O-tesuu o okake shimasu

Sorry for the trouble

❇ Used to express feelings of feeling sorry for the time and labor you are causing someone to spend on you.

POINT
- Often used with customers or those you are making requests of.
- Sometimes abbreviated "*o-tesuu desu ga.*"

---

❶ Work request

A：これを金曜日までに10個用意すればいいんですね。
B：そうです。**お手数をおかけします**。

A: So you need ten of these ready by Friday?
B: That's correct. Sorry for the trouble.

❷ A message

A：じゃ、田中先生にそう伝えておきますね。
B：はい。**お手数をおかけします**。

A: Then I'll let Tanaka-sensei know that.
B: Okay. Sorry for the trouble.

❸ Lost articles

A：**お手数をおかけします**が、もし見つかったら、お電話をいただけますか。
B：わかりました。

A: Sorry for the trouble, but if you find them, could you please call me?
B: Alright.

Variations

❹ Confirming receipt

A：先ほどFAXをお送りしました。**お手数ですが**、ご確認のほどよろしくお願いします。
B：はい、確かに受け取りました。

A: I sent a FAX earlier. Sorry for the trouble, but could you please confirm that it arrived?
B: Yes, it did arrive.

38 思ったとおり *Omotta toori*

Just as I thought

✿ When something goes exactly as predicted

POINT

➡ "*Omotta toori*", "*omotta toori*+*no*+N", "*omotta toori (ni)*+V" and other various shapes of this can be used.

---

❶ A kind person

A：その話を聞いて感心したよ。
B：**思ったとおり**。彼女はすごく優しい人なんだよ。

A: I thought that story was very admirable.
B: Just as I thought. She's a very kind person.

❷ Someone's idea

A：今回中止になったのは部長の意向なんだって。
B：**思ったとおり**。最初からやりたくなかったんだよ。

A: Stopping this time was the department chief's idea, apparently.
B: Just as I thought. He didn't want to do this to begin with.

❸ Made to order

A：いかがでしょうか。
B：わあ、**思ったとおり**です。こんな感じのが欲しかったんです。

A: How do you like it?
B: Wow, it's just like I thought it'd be. I wanted something like this.

❹ Hiring interview

A：面接、残念だったね。
B：人生、**思ったとおり**にはいかないよ。

A: It's too bad about the interview.
B: Life doesn't always go as you think it will, after all.

53

39 恩に着る *On ni kiru*

Indebted to

❀ A word used to show gratitude for an act someone did for you.

POINT
➡ An expression used to communicate feelings of "I will not forget your kindness and intend to repay you some day."

❶ Trading places

A：明日のバイト、代わり探してるんだって？代わろうか。
B：ほんと!? ありがとう、**恩に着る**よ。

A: I heard you were looking for someone to work in your place at your part-time job tomorrow? I can do it.
B: Really?! Thank you, I'm indebted to you.

❷ An introduction

A：じゃ、今度、森先生に紹介するね。
B：ありがとうございます。**恩に着ます**。

A: I'll introduce you to Mori-sensei in that case.
B: Thank you very much. I'm indebted to you.

❸ Helping out

A：それ、大変そうだね。ちょっと手伝おうか。
B：ほんとに!? **恩に着る**よ。

A: That looks tough. Could I help you out?
B: Really?! I'd be in your debt.

❹ In my place

A：明日、代わりに行ってくれたら、**恩に着る**んだけど。
B：悪いけど、ぼくも予定があるんだよ。

A: I'd be indebted to you if you could go in my place tomorrow.
B: Sorry, but I already have plans too.

40 カチンと来る *Kachin to kuru*

Pissed off, ~ be annoyed with, ~get on one's nerves

❁ **To feel unpleasant about someone's remark or attitude.**

POINT
➡ It is often used when the target is faced toward yourself.
➡ It is often used when the contents of an remark or expression are very rude or have no touch of delicacy.

❶ At the workplace

A：あの言い方には**カチンと来ました**。
B：まあまあ。大事な取引先だから。

A: I was very offended by what he said.
B: Well well, they are our important client…

❷ Making a fool out of someone

A：「君には難しいかも」って言われたんだって。
B：それは**カチンと来る**ね。

A: He was told, "It might be difficult for you to handle."
B: That is annoying!

❸ Between clerks

A：いくらお客さんだからって、あんな言い方はないよ。
B：**カチンと来る**よね。

A: That's no way of talking even if he is a customer.
B: You're right, it's very disgusting.

❹ Unreasonable

A：私一人が悪いみたいに言われて…。
B：それは**カチンと来る**ね。

A: It sounded as if I were the only one in the wrong…
B: That's annoying.

55

41 がっくり *Gakkuri*

Bummed out, down in the dumps, burned out

❀ To lose one's energy and feel depressed at once because the result is against your expectation or because of tough situations.

POINT
➡ It is a feeling of losing strength, and as if whatever that was straight breaks all of sudden.

❶ Failing an examination

A: 絶対受かると思ってたのに、**がっくり**だよ。
B: また、次頑張ればいいじゃない。

A: I was sure to pass the exam, so I'm pretty bummed out.
B: Cheer up, just try again.

❷ Rejection

A: 企画書、全然だめでした。**がっくり**です。
B: えっ、そうなんですか。

A: The project proposal was rejected. I feel down in the dumps.
B: What? Is that right?

❸ Unfortunate

A: 洗濯物、全部雨に濡れちゃってたよ。**がっくり**。
B: 今日、いきなり降り出したもんね。

A: Damn! The laundry was all wet because of the rain.
B: Yeah, today's rain was unexpected.

❹ Waste

A: せっかくケーキ買ったのに、落としちゃって。
B: それは**がっくり**だったね。

A: I went to the trouble of buying a cake, but I dropped it.
B: Aw, shucks, that's too bad.

42 かっこ悪い *Kakko warui*

Uncool; lame

1: When something does not look good because of its balance or condition being poor.
2: When an action or attitude is disgraceful.

POINT
➡ Also used to show feelings of embarrassment at a poor impression being given to others.

❶ An old coat

A：このコート、デザインが古くて、ちょっと**かっこ悪い**なあ。
B：そうでもないよ。

A: This coat has an old design, so it's a little uncool.
B: That's not true.

❷ The quality of a speech

A：いろいろ言い間違えて**かっこ悪かった**なあ。緊張してたから。
B：そう？ 上手だったよ。

A: I said a lot of things wrong and was really uncool. It's because I was nervous.
B: Really? You did well.

❸ Before a ceremony

A：遅れて行くの、ちょっと**かっこ悪い**けど、しょうがないか。
B：そうだね。

A: Going late is a little uncool, but what can you do.
B: That's right.

❹ After a musical performance

A：いつもはもっとうまく弾けるんだけど、騒がしくて気が散っちゃったよ。
B：言い訳するの、**かっこ悪い**よ。

A: I can usually play much better, but it was too noisy and I was distracted.
B: It's not cool to give excuses.

57

43 勝手にやれば？ *Katte ni yareba?*

Why don't you do it yourself?

🌸 Used to express a hostile feeling of "I don't care anymore, so do as you like" because you are shocked by someone's selfish attitude.

POINT
➡ *"Katte"* means "To do as one wants without considering their surroundings."

---

① Resignation

A: 納得できないなら、勝手にやれば？
B: じゃ、そうするよ。

A: If you're not going to be happy with it, why don't you do it yourself?
B: Okay, then I will.

Variations ---

② Freedom isn't always good

A: やりたい人が勝手にやればいいと思います。
B: そういうわけにもいかないよ。

A: I think people who want to do it can do it themselves.
B: It's not going to work out like that.

③ At home

A: 私がしたいんだから、反対しないでよ。
B: わかった。じゃあ、もう、勝手にしたら？

A: I want to do it, so stop opposing me.
B: Fine. Then why don't you go do it on your own?

④ A warning

A: 勝手にすればいいけど、人に迷惑かけたらだめだよ。
B: わかってます。

A: You can do as you want, but you shouldn't cause trouble to others.
B: I know.

44 勝手を言ってすみません
Katte o itte sumimasen

I'm sorry for my selfish request

❋ A phrase used to apologize because you feel bad for attempting to get your way despite what was planned or someone's expectations.

POINT
➡ Used to receive the understanding of others when asking a large favor.

❶ With a coach

A：じゃ、しばらく練習に来(ら)れないんですね。
B：はい。**勝手を言ってすみません**。

A: So you won't be able to come to practice for a while.
B: Yes. I'm sorry for my selfish request.

❷ At the workplace

A：あのう、**勝手を言ってすみません**が、来週の月曜、休みをいただいてもいいですか。
B：わかった。いいよ。

A: Um, I apologize for my selfish request, but may I take next Monday off?
B: Okay, it's fine.

Variations

❸ A job offer

A：そうか…だめか…。いい話だと思うんだけどね。
B：はい…。**勝手を言って申し訳ありません**。

A: I see... So you can't... I do think it's a good chance.
B: Yes... I'm sorry for my selfish request.

❹ Appointment

A：金曜は5時に駅前で大丈夫？
B：それなんですが、6時にしてもらえませんか。**勝手を言って申し訳ないんですが**。

A: 5 in front of the station okay for Friday?
B: About that, could we make it 6? I'm sorry for my selfish request.

45 変わらないです *Kawaranai desu*

The same (as always); hasn't changed

❀ 1: When a situation has not changed in a noticeable way
2: When there is no difference between multiple things.

POINT
➡ Whether or not the lack of change is good or bad depends on the situation, so it can be used as both a positive and a negative evaluation.

❶ A nostalgic spot

A：久しぶりに来たけど、昔と全然**変わらない**。
B：へー、そうなんだ。

A: It's been a while since I was here last, but it hasn't changed one bit since then.
B: Wow, really?

❷ At a clinic

A：ひざの調子はどうですか。
B：うーん。あまり**変わらないです**。

A: How is your knee feeling?
B: Hmm. It hasn't changed very much.

❸ On the phone

A：どうもご無沙汰しています。**お変わりないですか**。
B：はい、おかげさまで。

A: It's been a while. How are you, the same as always?
B: Yes, thanks to you.

❹ At the store

A：これはどう？
B：あっちの安いのとあんまり**変わらない**んじゃない？

A: How about this one?
B: Isn't it about the same as that cheap one over there?

46 考えられない *Kangaerarenai*

Unthinkable

❖ A phrase used to deny the possibility of something as a fact or a choice.

POINT
➡ A phrase used to show feelings of being unable to accept something.

❶ Cooking

A：砂糖と間違えて塩を入れるなんて…。**考えられない**。
B：すみません。

A: Accidentally putting in salt instead of sugar…? That's unthinkable.
B: I'm sorry.

❷ A poor workplace

A：毎日残業があるんだけど、残業代は出ないんです。
B：えっ、そうなの!? **考えられない**よ。

A: I have overtime everyday, but I'm not being paid for it.
B: What, really?! That's unthinkable.

❸ An unusual couple

A：まさか、あの二人が付き合ってるとか？
B：いや、それは**考えられない**よね。

A: Don't tell me those two are going out or something.
B: No, that'd be unthinkable.

❹ Living together with parents

A：一人暮らしするの？
B：いえ、病気の母を残して家を出るなんて、私には**考えられません**。

A: Are you going to live by yourself?
B: No, leaving my sick mother behind and leaving the house would be unthinkable.

47 関係ない *Kankee nai*

It doesn't matter

✿ Used to express that something isn't important or isn't a problem.

POINT
➡ Often used to tell someone worrying "There's no need to worry, don't be bothered by it."

❶ An interesting job

A：その仕事は経験がないとだめなんですか。
B：**関係ない**よ。

A: Do you need to have experience for that job?
B: It doesn't matter.

❷ The source of trouble

A：もしかして、私が言ったことがまずかった？
B：いやいや、それは**関係ない**よ。

A: Could I have said something wrong?
B: No, that doesn't have anything to do with it.

❸ About brands

A：ブランドとか気にする？
B：全然。自分の好みなら、ブランドとか**関係ない**よ。

A: Do you pay attention to brands?
B: Not at all. I don't care about brands as long as I like what I'm buying.

❹ An interesting job

A：こういう仕事だから、土日は**関係ない**んですよ。
B：そうですか。でも、面白そうですね。

A: Because the job is this way, I still have to work on Saturdays and Sundays.
B: Is that so. But it does seem interesting.

❺ Going my way

A：人がどう言おうが**関係ない**よ。自分がやりたいようにやればいいよ。
B：はい。

A: It doesn't matter what people say. Just do things how you want to do them.
B: Okay.

48 感心する *Kanshin suru*

I'm impressed

✿ To be moved by deep feelings as a result of coming across an incredible action, highly-advanced techniques, and so on.

POINT
➡ *"Kanshin shinai"* is used when you are unable to see something in a positive light.

---

❶ Handmade sweets

A：これ、よかったら食べて。
B：ありがとう。・・・リサさんが作るお菓子はいつもほんとにおいしくて**感心する**。

A: Please have some if you'd like.
B: Thank you... The sweets you make are always so delicious, I'm impressed, Lisa-san.

❷ Teacher and student

A：リンダさんは卒業するまで１度も授業を休まなかったんですね。**感心しました**。
B：いえいえ、先生の授業が楽しかったからですよ。

A: You didn't take a single day off of classes your entire time here, Linda-san. I'm impressed.
B: Not at all, I just enjoyed your classes, that's it.

❸ Together with feelings of respect

A：さくらさんってほんとポジティブだよね。**感心する**よ。
B：えっ、そうですか。

A: You're so positive, Sakura-san. I'm impressed.
B: What, really?

❹ How something is done

A：そういうやり方はあまり**感心しない**な。
B：…すみません。

A: I can't say I'm very impressed by that way of doing things.
B: ...I'm sorry.

63

49 勘弁して（ほしい） *Kanben shite (hoshii)*

Give me a break

✿ Used to express feelings of wanting someone to stop because you are troubled or made uncomfortable by their actions.

POINT

➡ "*Kanben suru*" means to let someone off, while "*kanben shite kudasai*" is used to ask for forgiveness.

---

❶ At the workplace

A：今日も残業になるみたい。
B：えー、また？ もう勘弁してほしいよ。

A: Looks like overtime today, as well.
B: What, again? Give me a break.

❷ On the phone

A：ごめん、今日も仕事で会えない。
B：もう勘弁してよ！ いつも直前に！

A: Sorry, I have work again today and can't meet.
B: Give me a break! You always do this right before!

❸ Long rain

A：また今日も雨だ。
B：また？ もう１週間だよ。ほんと勘弁してほしい。

A: It's raining again today.
B: Again? It's been a week now. I wish it'd let up.

Variations ---

❹ On a rollercoaster platform

A：ああ、楽しかった。もう１回乗る？
B：いや、もう勘弁…。

A: Wow, that was fun. Want to ride it again?
B: No, I think I've had enough...

50 聞いてない *Kiitenai*

I never heard about that

✿ Used to express feelings of surprise and dissatisfaction upon learning a fact or information.

POINT
➡ Often used when you haven't heard about changes in plans, etc.
➡ Includes feelings of shock at the fact you hadn't heard.

❶ A changed reservation

A：あのお客さん、予約は今日に変更したって言ってるんです。
B：本当ですか。聞いてませんよ。

A: That customer is saying she changed her reservation to today.
B: Really? I never heard about that.

❷ The President in attendance

A：社長が会議に出るなんて、聞いてませんよ。
B：私も聞いてないです。

A: I never heard that the president would be at the meeting.
B: Neither did I.

❸ A fee system

A：では、お食事代とお飲み物代で、あわせて9500円になります。
B：えっ？ 飲み物代が別なんて、聞いてないよ。

A: So your food and drink together comes out to 9,500 yen.
B: What? I never heard that food and drink were separate.

❹ A change in date

A：明日の会議の準備はもうできてる？
B：えっ、明日になったんですか！ 聞いてませんよ！

A: Are you ready for tomorrow's meeting?
B: What, it was changed to tomorrow?! I never heard about that!

❺ Who will be hosting

A：司会は田中さんがやるんだって？
B：えっ。何も聞いてないですよ！

A: I heard that you'll be hosting tomorrow, Tanaka-san?
B: What? I never heard about that!

51 気が重い *Ki ga omoi*

Feel down; feel depressed

❀ To feel depressed or uninterested in doing things because something is difficult or because you are not interested.

POINT
➡ Whatever makes one feel down is something that one tries to avoid if possible.

---

❶ Before test results are posted

A：合格発表はいつ？
B：明日。全然自信ないから、**気が重い**よ。

A: When do they announce who passed?
B: Tomorrow. I'm not confident at all, so I feel down.

❷ With friends on Sunday

A：また明日から仕事か…。
B：**気が重く**なるね。

A: Back to work tomorrow...
B: Makes you feel depressed, doesn't it?

❸ An unpleasant role

A：4月以降は契約ができないこと、本人に伝えといてくれる？
B：私がですか!? それはちょっと…**気が重い**です。

A: Could you tell him that we can't continue his contract from April?
B: Me?! That's a little...depressing.

❹ Plans for a work trip

A：来週、社長と出張？
B：そう。ちょっと**気が重く**なる。

A: You're going on a work trip with the president next week?
B: That's right. It has me a little down.

52 気が利くね *Ki ga kiku ne*

How thoughtful

❀ **Used to express feelings of admiration for someone paying attention to and being considerate of small details.**

POINT
➡ Used to speak of an action or attitude taken without being asked to make someone else happy or for their sake.

---

❶ Handing a throat drop to someone coughing

A：これ、よかったらどうぞ。
B：ありがとう。**気が利くね**。

A: If you'd like one, here you go.
B: Thank you. How thoughtful.

❷ A cup of coffee

A：お疲れ。コーヒーいれたよ。
B：さすがマイケル、**気が利くなあ**。

A: Good work. I made some coffee.
B: That's just like you, Michael, so thoughtful.

❸ Work

A：ちょっと、手伝ってよ！ **気が利かない**なあ。
B：ごめん、ごめん。

A: Hey, can you help out? You're so unthoughtful.
B: Sorry, sorry.

Variations

❹ 「気の利いたこと」

A：**気の利いたこと**は言えないけど、いつも応援してるから。
B：ありがとう。

A: I can't say anything thoughtful, but I'm always rooting for you.
B: Thank you.

53 気が気じゃなかった
Ki ga ki ja nakatta

Was on pins and needles

❀ To have been so concerned about something that you were unable to calm down.

POINT
➡ Indicates feelings of having being worried and unable to stay mentally calm about how something you were anxious about would proceed.

---

❶ After getting test results

A：検査の結果が出るまで、**気が気じゃなかった**です。
B：大きな病気じゃなくて、安心しましたね。

A: I was on pins and needles until those test results came back.
B: It's a good thing that it wasn't a major illness.

❷ At the workplace

A：いつ社長が怒りだすか、ハラハラしたね。
B：ほんと。**気が気じゃなかった**よ。

A: My heart was thumping because I didn't know when the President would get mad.
B: Really. I was on pins and needles.

❸ Keeping a secret from your parents

A：いつ親に知られるか、**気が気じゃなかった**よ。
B：結局、大丈夫だったの？

A: I was on pins and needles wondering if my parents would find out.
B: So, was it okay in the end?

❹ Getting home late

A：昨日は、娘が夜11時まで帰ってこなくて。
B：それは、**気が気じゃなかった**ですね。

A: My daughter didn't come home until 11 at night yesterday.
B: You must have been on pins and needles.

54 気が進まない *Ki ga susumanai*

Not in the mood

❀ Used to express feelings of being unable to do something assertively.

POINT

➡ Often used to talk about something you are uninterested in or something that must be done despite your wishes.

---

❶ A party

A：青木さんはパーティーに行かないの？
B：うん…。あんまり気が進まなくて。

A: Are you not going to the party, Aoki-san?
B: No... I'm not really in the mood to go.

❷ Training

A：研修受けてみたら？
B：ちょっと専門的すぎる気がして、今一つ気が進まないんだよ。

A: Why don't you try doing some training?
B: I feel like it's too specialized, so I can't get into the mood.

❸ Having to warn people

A：部長が君に、田中さんに注意してくれって。
B：私が？　気が進まないなあ。

A: The chief said for you to warn Tanaka-san.
B: Me? I feel reluctant to do that.

Variations -

❹ An invitation

A：気が進んだときでいいんだけど、今度一緒に山登りに行かない？
B：はい。じゃ、いつか。

A: We can go when you're in the mood, but would you like to climb a mountain together with me next time?
B: Yes, let's go some time.

55 聞かなかったことにして

Kikanakatta koto ni shite

Pretend you didn't hear that

❋ An expression used to ask someone to not repeat something heard when they were not supposed to hear it or when it is supposed to be kept a secret.

POINT

➡ Similar expressions include "*minakatta koto ni shite kudasai*" and "*nakatta koto ni shite kudasai.*"

❶ Something not public yet

A：さっき聞こえちゃったんだけど、会社、やめちゃうの？
B：うん。でも、とりあえず聞かなかったことにしてね。

A: I just overheard you, but you're quitting the company?
B: Yes. But pretend you didn't hear that for now.

❷ Something worrying

A：聞かなかったことにしてほしいんだけど、昨日、リサさん、泣いてた。
B：えっ？　どうしたんだろう？　心配だね。

A: I want you to pretend you never heard this, but Lisa-san was crying yesterday.
B: What? What could have happened? That's worrying.

❸ True feelings

A：本当はあの人、嫌いなんだよね。
B：え？
A：うそうそ。聞かなかったことにして。

A: I actually don't like that person.
B: What?
A: Just kidding. Pretend you didn't hear that.

Related phrases ----------

❹ 「なかったことにして」

A：この前言ってたパーティー、いつやるの？　早くやろうよ。
B：ごめん、あれはなかったことにして。

A: When are you going to have that party you were talking about the other day? Let's hurry up and do it.
B: Sorry, pretend you didn't hear about that.

56 気が向いたら（でいい）

Ki ga muitara (de ii)

You can if you feel interested

❀ **An expression used to casually tell someone who you are inviting or making a request of that "You can do it if you like."**

POINT

▶▶ *"Ki ga muku"* means "To feel like doing that."

---

❶ An invitation

A：そのお店、今度、森さんも一緒に行こうよ。
B：そうだねえ…。まあ、気が向いたら。

A: Let's go to that store together next time, Mori-san.
B: You're right... Well, if you feel interested.

❷ Exercise suggestions

A：何か体を動かすことをしたほうがいいんじゃない？
B：うん、気が向いたらね。

A: Don't you think I ought to do something to move my body?
B: Yes, if you feel like it.

❸ When parting ways

A：また、連絡しますね。
B：ええ。気が向いたらでいいですよ。

A: I'll contact you again.
B: Yes, you can whenever you feel interested.

❹ At an office

A：気が向いたらでいいから、この資料に目を通してみて。
B：わかりました。

A: Could you take a look over these materials? You can do it whenever you feel interested.
B: I understand.

57 期待してたんだけど
Kitai shiteta n dakedo

I had my hopes up

❋ Used to express feelings of regret that things did not go as expected.

POINT
➡ What goes after "*kitai shiteta n dakedo*" is frequently omitted.

❶ At a restaurant
A：評判いい店だから、**期待してたんだけど**。
B：思ったより普通だったね。

A: I had my hopes up because it was a good store, but...
B: It was more average than I'd expected.

❷ After seeing a movie
A：なんか、がっかりだったね
B：うん。予告見て**期待してたんだけど**なあ。

A: I feel kind of let down, don't you?
B: Yes. And I had my hopes up after seeing the trailer.

❸ At the workplace
A：この商品には**期待してたんだけど**ね。
B：うん。売れ行き、あんまりよくないみたいですね。

A: I had my hopes up for this product.
B: Yes. It doesn't seem to be selling very well.

Variations

❹ After seeing a sports match
A：優勝、**期待してたのに**なあ。
B：まさか最初の試合に負けるとはね。

A: I had my hopes up for a win.
B: I never thought they'd lose their first match.

58 きついです *Kitsui desu*

It's rough; tight

✿ 1: When something is extreme in degree and not easily withstood.
2: When something is tight with little margin.

POINT

➡ The opposite of "*kitsui*" is "*yurui*". Used when a situation is tough and difficult, not laid back and peaceful.

❶ With a friend

A：新しい職場はどう？
B：仕事は**きつい**けど、やりがいあるよ。

A: How is your new workplace?
B: The work is rough, but it's worth doing.

❷ Not getting better

A：風邪、長引いてるね。大丈夫？
B：さすがにちょっと**きついです**ね。

A: You've had a cold for a while. Are you okay?
B: I have to admit, it's a little rough.

❸ At the workplace

A：部長、言い方は**きつい**けど、本当はいい人なんだよ。
B：ええ、わかってます。

A: The department chief can say some rough things, but he's actually a good person.
B: Yes, I know.

❹ Trying on a skirt

A：お客様、いかがですか。
B：ちょっと**きついです**。

A: How is it, miss?
B: It's a little tight.

59 気に入った *Ki ni itta*

~ love it, ~like it

🌸 Have favorable impression because it suits one's emotions or feelings.

POINT
➡ You read it "*iru*" instead of "*hairu*" in this case " 入る ".
➡ The opposite of "*ki ni iru*" is "*ki ni iranai.*"

❶ A present
A：何がいいか、迷ったんだけど…。
B：ありがとう。すごく気に入ったよ。

A: I wondered what to get…
B: Thank you so much. I really love it.

❷ At the store
A：どれか気に入った？
B：うん、この赤いコートが。

A: Anything you like?
B: Yeah, this red coat.

❸ At the Restaurant
A：この店、気に入ったよ。
B：うん。雰囲気いいし、おいしいしね。

A: This restaurant is awesome.
B: Yes, the atmosphere is wonderful, and so is the food.

❹ View
A：どうしてこの部屋にしたんですか。
B：ここからの景色が気に入ったんです。

A: Why did you choose this room?
B: I really liked the view from here.

Related phrases

❺ 「お気に入り」
A：いつもそのペン使ってるね。
B：うん。書きやすくてお気に入りなんだ。

A: You're always using that pen.
B: Yep, it's very easy to write, and it's my favorite.

60 気に障ったらごめんなさい
Ki ni sawattara gomennasai

Sorry if I rubbed you the wrong way

❋ An expression used to show that you feel sorry if your own words or actions caused displeasure to others.

POINT
➡ Often used after words or actions that may cause displeasure to others, but sometimes said in advance of them.

❶ An incorrect character

A：気に障ったらごめんなさいね。この字、間違ってますよ。
B：あ、本当だ。ありがとうございます。

A: Sorry if this rubs you the wrong way, but this character is wrong.
B: Oh, you're right. Thank you.

❷ An addendum

A：さっき言ったのは悪い意味じゃないからね。気に障ったらごめん。
B：大丈夫、気にしてないよ。

A: I didn't mean what I said in a negative way. Sorry if that rubbed you the wrong way.
B: It's fine, don't worry.

❸ An honest opinion

A：ご主人、ちょっと冷たくない？ …あっ、気に障ったらごめんね。
B：ううん、実際そうだから。優しいところもあるんだけどね。

A: Isn't your husband a little cold? ...Oh, sorry if that rubbed you the wrong way.
B: No, it's true. He does have a kind side too, though.

❹ Thoughts on someone's clothes

A：気に障ったらごめん。その服、ちょっと地味じゃない？
B：これ？ やっぱりそう思う？

A: Sorry if this rubs you the wrong way, but aren't those clothes a little plain?
B: These? Do you think so, after all?

❺ Why there are many mistakes

A：気に障ったらごめんなさい。最近ミスが多いけど、何か悩みでもあるの？
A：うん、ちょっと…。

A: Sorry of this rubs you the wrong way, but you've been making a lot of mistakes lately. Is something troubling you?
B: Well, kind of...

75

61 気になる *Ki ni naru*

Bothers me; worries me; interested in

❀ When one cannot feel at ease because they cannot take their mind off of something.

POINT
➡ "*Ki ni naru*" is an intransitive verb, while "*ki ni suru*" is a transitive verb.

---

❶ While working

A：ねえ、気になるからテレビ消して。
B：えー、今いいところなのに。

A: Hey, could you turn the TV off? It's bothering me.
B: What? But it's just getting to a good part.

❷ With a friend

A：結婚相手の収入って気になる？
B：それはやっぱりねえ。

A: Is your fiancé's salary something you're interested in?
B: You know, it really does.

❸ A strange smell

A：なんかにおわない？
B：うん、少し気になったけど、気のせいかなって…。

A: Does something smell funny?
B: Yeah, it was bothering me a little, but I thought it could just be my imagination...

❹ A new store

A：今度 ABC カフェ行かない？
B：ああ、あそこ、私も気になってた！

A: Do you want to try going to ABC Café next time?
B: Oh, I was interested in going there too!

62 気のせい *Ki no see*

(Your / my) imagination

❋ When something feels different from reality for no specific reason.

POINT
➡ "*Ki*" in this case means "A figment of someone's imagination vaguely felt for no reason."

❶ Someone's voice?

A：今、女の人の声が聞こえなかった？
B：え、**気のせい**だよ。怖いこと言わないで。

A: Did you just hear a woman's voice?
B: Huh? That was your imagination. Stop saying such scary things.

❷ Do I have a fever?

A：**気のせい**かなあ…。熱があるかもしれない。
B：ほんと？ ちゃんと測ったら？

A: Maybe it's just my imagination...but I might have a fever.
B: Really? Why don't you take your temperature?

❸ Cold?

A：今日、なんか寒くない？ **気のせい**？
B：うーん。暖かいほうだと思うけど。風邪じゃない？

A: Does it feel cold to you today? Is it just my imagination?
B: Hmm. If anything, it feels warm to me. Maybe you have a cold?

❹ Is it just me?

A：部長、私にだけ厳しくない？
B：そんなことないって。**気のせい**だよ。

A: Is the department chief especially hard on just me?
B: I told you, that's not true. It's just your imagination.

77

63 決まってる *Kimatteru*

Of course

❋ An expression used to emphasize the certainty of a matter. Used in some cases when something is common knowledge, but it can also be used based on the speaker's personal convictions.

POINT

➡ While simply "*kimatteru*" can be used when replying in the affirmative to someone's question, "~ *nai ni kimatteru*" is used when replying in the negative.

---

❶ A sneak preview of a film

A：映画、見に行く？
B：**決まってる**でしょ！ 無料招待なんだから。

A: Do you want to go see the movie?
B: Of course! It's a free ticket.

❷ A famous restaurant

A：ここ、すごくおいしいね！
B：**決まってる**じゃない！ 超有名な店だよ。

A: This place is delicious!
B: Of course! It's a super-famous store.

❸ At a banquet

A：お酒、全然飲まないの？
B：ダメに**決まってる**じゃない！ 運転するんだから。

A: Are you not going to drink at all?
B: Of course I can't! I'm going to be driving.

❹ About a friend

A：彼女、英語しゃべれるの？
B：**決まってる**でしょ。高校までずっとハワイだよ。

A: Can she speak English?
B: Of course she can. She lived in Hawaii all the way until high school.

64 気持ちいい *Kimochi ii*

Feel so good

❋ This describes physical or mental comfortableness.

POINT
- "*Kimochi ga ii*" can also be said.
- This can also refer to people's attitude or behavior.

① In a hot spring

A：あ〜気持ちいい。
B：温泉は最高だね。

A: Ah, I feel so good.
B: Nothing is better than hot springs.

② On a sunny day

A：久しぶりに晴れたね。
B：うん、すごく気持ちいい。

A: We finally got some sunshine.
B: Yes, it feels so good.

③ In an interview with an athlete

A：優勝おめでとうございます！ 今のお気持ちは？
B：最高に気持ちいいです！

A: Congratulations on your victory! How do you feel?
B: I feel so good!

Variations

④ Watching a match

A：お互い全力を出し合って、見ていて気持ちがいいですね。
B：そうですね。

A: Both teams did their best. It's invigorating to watch.
B: That's true.

65 気持ち悪い *Kimochi warui*

Feel sick, unpleasant. Feel bad.

❋ It describes physical, instinctive unpleasantness or psychological antipathy.

POINT
- "*Kimochi ga warui*" can also be said.
- It also refers to people's appearance, attitude, situation, etc.

---

❶ In a car
A：あ、ちょっと酔ったかも。**気持ち悪い**。
B：大丈夫？ 車停めようか。

A: Ah, I'm carsick. I feel bad.
B: Are you okay? Do you want me to stop the car?

❷ An insect
A：あ、なんか変な虫。
B：ほんとだ、**気持ち悪い**。

A: Look, there is a strange insect.
B: True. It's horrible.

❸ A suspicious-looking man
A：あの人、ずっとこっち見てて**気持ち悪い**。
B：なんか怪しいね。気をつけてよ。

A: That man has been staring at us. He looks weird.
B: He's a bit creepy. You should be careful.

❹ At home
A：すごい汗。大丈夫？
B：ちょっと**気持ち悪い**夢見ちゃって…。

A: You are sweating a lot. Are you all right?
B: I had a scary dream….

❺ With a friend
A：その髪型…。あ、何でもない。
B：何？ 最後まで言ってよ！ **気持ち悪い**じゃない。

A: Your hairstyle…. Whoops… nothing.
B: What? What were you going to say? I don't feel too good.

66 急な話で恐縮ですが
きゅう　はなし　きょうしゅく

Kyuuna hanashi de kyooshuku desuga

I apologize for suddenly bringing this up

❋ An expression used to introduce a question, report, or so on without prior notification. Used to express feelings of thanks and apology.

POINT

➤ Primarily used when saying something that could mildly surprise someone or that requires an immediate response from them.

❶ Invitation to a wedding ceremony

A：あのう、**急な話で恐縮ですが**、来月結婚することになりまして、ぜひ式にご出席いただきたいのですが…。

B：おお、それはおめでとう。もちろん、出席しますよ。

A: Um, I apologize for suddenly bringing this up, but I'm going to get married next year, and I'd like you to attend the ceremony...

B: Oh, congratulations! Of course I'll attend.

❷ Comments when leaving a company

A：**急な話で恐縮ですが**、今月いっぱいで会社をやめることになりました。

B：えっ、やめちゃうの!? そうか…残念だなあ。

A: I apologize for suddenly bringing this up, but I'll be quitting the company at the end of this month.

B: What, you're quitting?! Oh...that's too bad.

Variations

❸ On the phone

A：**急な話で悪いんだけど**、今日、午後からシフトに入れない？

B：午後からですか!? わかりました。

A: I apologize for suddenly bringing this up, but would you like to work a shift starting this afternoon?

B: From this afternoon?! Alright.

❹ Cancellation

A：あの、**急な話で申し訳ないんですが**、午後の予約をキャンセルしてもらえませんか。

B：わかりました。１時の予約をキャンセルですね。

A: Um, I apologize for suddenly bringing this up, but could you please cancel my afternoon reservation?

B: I understand. So you would like me to cancel your 1 o'clock reservation?

67 急に言われても困る
Kyuuni iwaretemo komaru

You can't suddenly say that

❋ The state of not knowing how to respond when something is suddenly requested of you or reported to you.

POINT
➡ Abbreviations such as 「急に言われても…」「急に言われてもね」 are also frequently used.

---

❶ On the phone, to your wife

A：今日、夕飯に同僚誘ってもいい？
B：えっ？ **急に言われても困る**よ。

A: Can I invite a coworker to dinner tonight?
B: What? You can't suddenly say that.

❷ A sudden request

A：あとで二人を迎えに行ってあげてくれない？
B：えー、**急に言われても困る**よ。私だって用事があるんだから。

A: Could you pick two up for me later?
B: What? You can't suddenly say that. I have my own plans, too.

Variations

❸ Bored

A：ねえ、何か話してよ。何でもいいから。
B：えっ？ そんなこと**急に言われても**…。

A: Hey, talk to me about something. It doesn't matter what.
B: Huh? You can't suddenly say that and expect me to come up with something...

❹ Entering a hospital

A：検査には入院が必要ですが、今日、午後から大丈夫ですか。
B：えっ、入院ですか!? **急に言われても**…。

A: You'll need to be admitted to the hospital for the tests, but is tomorrow afternoon alright?
B: What? I need to be admitted? You can't suddenly say that...

68 今日はここまでにしましょう
きょう

Kyoo wa kokomade ni shimashoo

Let's stop here for today

✿ Used to communicate the intention to stop talking or working and continue what is currently being done at a later date.

POINT

▶ Primarily used by the person leading work.

---

❶ At school

A：**今日はここまでにしましょう**。明日は次の8課をやりますので、予習しておいてください。

B：わかりました。

A: Let's stop here for today. We'll do the next chapter, chapter 8, tomorrow, so please review it.

B: Alright.

❷ At the workplace

A：**今日はここまでにしよう**。お疲れ様。

B：お疲れ様でした。

A: Let's stop here for today. Good work.

B: Good work today.

Variations

❸ At the workplace

A：じゃ、**今日のところはここまでにしましょう**。次回、また続きをやりたいと思います。

B：お疲れ様でした。

A: Alright, let's stop here for today. I'd like to pick up where we left off next time.

B: Good work today.

❹ Work at home

A：明日も早いから、**今日はここまでにしとこうか**。

B：そうだね。

A: I need to be awake early again tomorrow, so let's stop here for today.

B: You're right.

83

69 気楽に *Kiraku ni*

Take it easy; easygoing; happy-go-lucky; not so serious

❀ Take it easy without worrying or taking things seriously.

POINT
➡ "*Kiraku*" is a state without any feeling of tension. Therefore, in some cases "*kiraku*" is used to mildly accuse someone of being "irresponsible, selfish."

❶ Worried

A：失敗したらどうしよう。
B：大丈夫。もっと**気楽に**いこう。

A: What should I do if I fail?
B: No worries. Take it easy.

❷ In front of a movie theater

A：どれがいい？
B：**気楽に**見られるのがいいな。

A: Which one do you want to see?
B: Let's see something light.

❸ A convenient app

A：このアプリ知ってた？
B：うん、使ってるよ。海外の人とも**気楽に**話せていいよね。

A: Do you know this app?
B: Yes, I'm using it. We can talk with people overseas easily.

❹ At the office

A：もう帰ろう。明日頑張ればいいよ。
B：ちょっと**気楽に**考えすぎじゃない？

A: Let's go home now. We can finish it tomorrow.
B: You sound like you're not taking it seriously, no?

70 きりがない *Kiri ga nai*

There's no end to it

✿ Used when something continues without end to express feelings of amazement, compromise, resignation, or shock.

POINT

➡ Frequently used together with expressions of assumption such as "~ *tara*" and "~*ba*."

---

❶ Better conditions

A：もっと給料が高くて、もっと楽で、もっと上司が優しい会社ないかな。

B：上を見たら、**きりがない**よ。

A: I wonder if there's a company out there with better pay, easier work, and kinder bosses.
B: If you start hoping for something better, there'll be no end to it.

❷ Before a speech

A：スピーチ、うまくできなかったらどうしよう。忘れるかもしれないし…。

B：心配しても**きりがない**よ。思い切ってやればいいよ。

A: What'll I do if the speech doesn't go well? I might forget it, too...
B: If you start worrying, there'll be no end to it. Just go out there and give it your all.

❸ A theme

A：それを議論し出すと**きりがない**からやめておこう。

B：そうですね。

A: If you bring this up as a topic to discuss, there'll be no end to it. Don't bother.
B: You're right.

❹ A design

A：やっと固まってきましたね。一応、ほかの色も見てみますか。

B：いいよ、**きりがない**から。

A: It's finally coming together. Why don't we try looking at other colors, though?
B: It's fine. There'll be no end to it.

85

71 具合はどう? *Guai wa doo?*

How do you feel? How are you?

❋ It is an expression used to inquire the status of things or of one's health condition.

POINT

➡ It is often used when inquiring how things are after there was a problem or something abnormal with human body or a machine.

---

❶ Physical Condition

A：**具合はどう？** 昨日は熱が出たって聞いてたけど。

B：おかげさまで、なんとか。

A: How do you feel? I heard that you had a fever yesterday.
B: Thank you, I'm feeling better.

❷ Injuries

A：けがの**具合はどう**ですか。

B：大丈夫ですよ。もう、ほとんど痛みもありません。

A: How is your injury coming along?
B: I'm doing ok, thank you. I hardly have any more pain.

❸ At the hospital

A：先生、祖母の**具合はどう**なんでしょうか。

B：1週間ほど入院すれば、よくなると思いますよ。

A: Doctor, how is my grandmother doing?
B: She'll be fine if she's in the hospital for a week.

❹ After repairing

A：エンジンの**具合はどう**ですか。

B：だいぶよくなりましたよ。

A: How is the engine?
B: Thanks, it's gotten much better.

Related phrases

❺「〜具合」

A：新幹線の混み**具合**は、どうでしたか。

B：自由席でも、座れるくらいでしたよ。

A: How crowded was the "shinkansen" bullet train?
B: The non-reserved seats were open, too.

72 くよくよしないで *Kuyokuyo shinai de*

Don't fret over, don't brood over, don't worry about

❖ It is an expression used for encouraging someone, telling them not to fret and worry over something forever.

POINT

➡ "*Kuyokuyo*" is a kind of mimetic word, while "*kuyokuyo suru*" means to keep minding and worrying over one's failure.

❶ After a failure

A：もう自信なくなったよ。また失敗する気がする。
B：そんなに**くよくよしないで**、元気出して。

A: I lost my confidence. I feel like I'm going to fail again.
B: Cheer up! Don't worry so much.

❷ After a failure

A：一回ミスしたくらいで、**くよくよするな**よ。
B：そうね。わかった。

A: Don't worry so much over one mistake.
B: Yeah, you're right. Ok.

Related phrases

❸「くよくよすることない」

A：そんなことで**くよくよすることない**んじゃない？
B：ほかの人には、ぼくの気持ちはわからないよ。

A: It's not anything to fret over, is it?
B: No one understands how I feel.

❹「くよくよしてもしょうがない」

A：いつまでも**くよくよしてもしょうがない**よ。
B：だって…。

A: It's no use crying over spilt milk.
B: But…

73 検討します *Kentoo shimasu*

Let me think it over

🌸 This coveys the speaker's intention to consider, avoid giving an immediate decision, and think it over.

POINT
➡ Even when the speaker takes a negative view, this fact is not said, and the decision is often held off by saying *"Kentoo shimasu."*
➡ A more formal expression than *"kangaemasu."*

❶ At a store

A: 今なら、さらに10%安くなります。
B: うーん…ちょっと**検討します**。

A: You can get a further 10% discount.
B: Uh…let me think it over.

❷ At a travel agent

A: この３つのプランはどれもおすすめです。
B: わかりました。ちょっと家族と**検討します**。

A: I recommend all these three plans.
B: Okay. I will discuss it with my family.

❸ About a business proposal

A: 何度もすみませんね。もうちょっと**検討させて**もらえますか。
B: わかりました。では、お返事お待ちしております。

A: I'm sorry to say this again, but let me think it over.
B: Okay. I am looking forward to hearing your reply.

❹ When shopping

A: ちょっと高いけど、これ、買っちゃおうか。
B: えー、もうちょっとよく**検討して**からにしようよ。

A: It's a bit expensive, but shall we buy it?
B: Uh, let's think it over.

74 誤解です *Gokai desu*

You're mistaken

✿ **Used to convey that someone has a mistaken understanding of something.**

POINT
➡ Often used when someone misunderstands something in a way that causes them to dislike you.
➡ Often used to clear up a misunderstanding and improve relations.

❶ Whose fault?

A：私のことが嫌いだから、そんなこと言うんでしょ。
B：えっ!? それは**誤解だよ**。

A: You're saying that because you don't like me, right?
B: What?! You're mistaken.

❷ Not enough trust

A：ビルさんって、いまいち信用できないんだよな。
B：ひどいなあ、**誤解ですよ**。

A: I just can't put much trust in you, Bill-san.
B: That's a terrible thing to say. You're mistaken.

❸ Who?

A：さっき一緒に歩いてた人は誰？
B：**誤解だよ**！ あれは妹だよ。

A: Who was that you were just walking with?
B: You're mistaken! That's my little sister.

❹ Reason for anger

A：どうして怒ってるのかよくわかりませんが、**誤解ですよ**。
B：えっ？ 何がですか。

A: I don't know why you're angry, but it's a misunderstanding.
B: What? What is?

89

75 ここだけの話ですが
Kokodake no hanashi desuga

Just between you and me; This stays here

✿ Used to express feelings that what is about to be said should be kept secret and not be repeated in other places.

POINT
➡ Other expressions with the same meaning include 「これは秘密ですが」 and 「これは内緒の話ですが」.

❶ Singing talent
A：歌うまいね！びっくり！
B：**ここだけの話ですが**、昔は歌手になりたかったんです。

A: You're good at singing! Wow!
B: Just between you and me, I once wanted to become a singer.

❷ Marriage
A：まだ**ここだけの話ですが**、課長と結婚することになりました。
B：えっ、いつから付き合ってたの!? 全然気づかなかった。

A: This stays here for now, but I'm going to be marrying the section chief.
B: What, how long have you been going out!? I never noticed.

Variations

❸ An unexpected side
A：**ここだけの話**、アニメとかゲームとか大好きなんです。
B：えっ、そうなんですか!? 意外です。

A: Just between you and me, I really like anime and games.
B: What, you do!? I didn't expect that.

❹ Uninterested
A：**ここだけの話**、ぼくはサッカーにはそんなに興味がないんです。
B：私もです。みんなに合わせてますけど。

A: This stays here, but I'm not that interested in soccer.
B: Me neither. I just go along with everyone else.

76 言葉も出ない　*Kotoba mo denai*

Nothing to say

❄ **Because the surprise and sensation is so huge, that you can't find an appropriate expression right away.**

POINT
- Used for both good and bad things.
- There are many expressions like "*kotoba ga denai*," "*kotoba mo nai*" or "*kotoba o ushinau*."

❶ Unexpected couple

A：あの二人が結婚するなんて…。
B：あまりに驚いて、**言葉も出なかった**よ。

A: Never dreamed those two would get married…
B: I'm so shocked that I have nothing to say.

❷ Impression on a movie

A：あまりの感動に、**言葉も出なかった**よ。
B：へえ、そんなによかったんだ。

A: That movie was so touching, I can't find the words.
B: Oh? Was it that good?

❸ About a colleague

A：仕事の途中で帰っちゃうなんて。
B：あきれて、**言葉も出ない**ね。

A: To leave in middle of work…
B: I'm too shocked to say a word.

Related phrases

❹ 「返す言葉もない」

A：勉強しなくて、受かるはずないでしょう。
B：そう言われると、**返す言葉もない**よ。

A: How would you ever pass without studying?
B: I'm speechless.

❺ 「言葉が見つからない」

A：まさか、突然亡くなるなんて…。**言葉が見つかりません**。
B：ええ、本当に。

A: Who would have expected he would pass away all of a sudden. I don't know what to say.
B: Yes, me neither.

77 子どもじゃないんだから

Kodomo ja nai n dakara

You're not a child

✿ Used to tell someone that as an adult, they ought to act the way an adult should act.

POINT
➡ Used to criticize someone's selfish attitude or behavior.

❶ At home

A：野菜、好きじゃないんだよね。
B：**子どもじゃないんだから**、好き嫌いしないで。

A: I just don't like vegetables.
B: You're not a child, don't be so picky.

❷ At the workplace

A：あの人、好きじゃないんですよ。
B：**子どもじゃないんだから**、好き嫌いで仕事はできないよ。

A: I don't like him.
B: You're not a child, so you can't pick who you work with based on whether you like them or not.

❸ At the workplace

A：田中さん、注意されるとすぐ泣くよね。
B：しっかりしてほしいよね、**子どもじゃないんだから**。

A: Tanaka-san cries as soon as you caution her.
B: I wish she'd be more composed. She's not a child.

❹ At home

A：**子どもじゃないんだから**、もうちょっと部屋を片付けたら？
B：時間がないんだよ。

A: You're not a child, can't you keep your room a little tidier?
B: I don't have time.

78 ご迷惑じゃないですか

Go-meewaku janai desu ka

Am I bothering you

🌸 A phrase used to show that one wishes to check whether their actions are causing problems for or bothering others.

POINT

➡ Used to show a modest attitude when someone offers to do something for your sake.

❶ Dinner invitation

A：よかったら、夕飯うちで食べて行って。
B：いいんですか。**ご迷惑じゃないですか**。

A: If you'd like, please come eat dinner at our home.
B: Is that alright? Would it not be a bother?

❷ Bring your child

A：マイケル君もパーティーに連れてきてくださいね。
B：え？ でも、**ご迷惑じゃないですか**。

A: Please bring Michael-kun to the party too.
B: What? Wouldn't that bother you?

Variations ---------------------------------

❸ Getting a ride

A：送ってもらってすみません。**ご迷惑じゃなかったですか**。
B：帰り道だから。気にしないで。

A: Thank you for giving me a ride. Was I not a bother?
B: This was on the way home. Don't worry about it.

❹ On the phone

A：毎日電話しちゃってごめんね。**迷惑じゃない？**
B：全然。私も楽しいよ。

A: Sorry for calling every day. Am I not bothering you?
B: Not at all. I enjoy it too.

79 これでいい? *Korede ii?*

Is this okay?

✿ An expression used to confirm whether something that has been prepared meets someone's demands.

POINT

➡ This becomes "*Kore de yoroshii deshoo ka.*" when said politely.

---

❶ Types of batteries

A：えーっと、電池って、**これでいい？**
B：そうそう、それ。

A: Um, is this battery okay?
B: Yes, that's the one.

❷ Writing instruments

A：何か、書くものない？
B：あるよ。**これでいい？**

A: Do you have something I could write with?
B: Yes. Is this okay?

Variations

❸ Materials for a meeting

A：午後の会議の資料なんですが、**これでよろしいでしょうか**。
B：ああ、いいよ。人数分コピー頼む。

A: About the materials for this afternoon's meeting. Are these alright?
B: Yes, those are okay. Could you please make copies for everyone attending?

❹ Types of cups

A：コップ、いくつかあるけど。
B：あ、**これでいいよ**。ありがとう。

A: We have a number of cups.
B: Oh, this one is okay. Thank you.

❺ Wiping a table

A：何か、拭くものない？
B：えっと、**これで大丈夫？**

A: Do you have anything I could use for wiping?
B: Um, is this okay?

80 こんなチャンスはめったにない

Konna chansu wa mettani nai

There aren't many chances like this

🌸 Used to say that it is extremely rare to have a certain opportunity and that it should therefore not be missed.

POINT

➡ Other expanded ways of saying this include "*Konna chansu, mettani nai kara, ~suru.*" and "*Konna chansu, mettani nai noni ~ teshimatta.*"

❶ A feeling of expectation

A：すぐ近くでオリンピックなんて、ワクワクするね。

B：うん。**こんなチャンスはめったにない**から、絶対見に行かなきゃ。

A: Isn't it exciting that the Olympics will be happening so close by?

B: Yes. There aren't many chances like this one, so I have to go see it.

❷ Appearing on TV

A：テレビに出るんだって？

B：うん。**こんなチャンス、めったにない**からね。

A: I heard you're going to be on TV?

B: Yes. There aren't many chances like this.

❸ At an autograph session for a popular athlete

A：サインもらわなくていいの？

B：うん…。たくさん並んでて時間かかりそうだから。

A：**こんなチャンス、めったにない**よ。待ってるから行っておいで。

A: Do you not need a signature?

B: Hmm… Well, the line is so long it seems like it would take a while.

A: There aren't many chances like this one. I'll wait here, you should go.

Related phrases

❹「こんな機会はめったにない」

A：村上春樹の講演会？　すごいじゃない！

B：そうなんだよ。**こんな機会はめったにない**から絶対行くよ。

A: A talk by Haruki Murakami? That's incredible!

B: That's right. There aren't many chances like this one, so I'm definitely going.

95

81 こんなもんじゃない？

Konnamon janai?

Isn't that (about) what you'd expect?; Is it any surprise?

❋ Used to express feelings that while it may not be sufficient, something is satisfying enough given the conditions.

POINT
- As this contains feelings of insufficiency, it is not used as a term of praise.
- *"Konnamono janai desu ka."* is used when saying politely.

❶ A cheap computer

A：このパソコン、ちょっと立ちあがりが遅いんだよな。
B：安かったし、まあ、こんなもんじゃない？

A: This computer takes a bit of time to boot up.
B: It was cheap, isn't that about what you'd expect?

❷ At a concert hall

A：やっぱり遠くてよく見えないね。
B：普通の席だからね。こんなもんじゃない？

A: After all, these were far and hard to see from.
B: Well, these were regular seats. Is it any surprise?

❸ Fancy wine

A：このワイン、ちょっと高すぎない？
B：でも高級なやつだし、こんなもんじゃない？

A: Isn't this wine a little too expensive?
B: Well, it is a fancy one. Isn't that about what you'd expect?

❹ Watching a sports match

A：結局、負けちゃったね。前半はリードしたのにね。
B：ま、こんなもんじゃない？ 実力だよ。

A: We ended up losing, even though we were in the lead during the first half.
B: But can you be surprised? It's all about talent.

82 最高 *Saikoo*

It's amazing; It's the best

❉ Used to indicate that something is so incredible that it could not be any greater.

POINT
- Often used after asked for one's opinion.
- A more straightforward expression of being moved or excited than terms such as *"totemo yokatta."*

❶ The scenery
A：わあ、すごい景色！
B：ここからの眺めは、最高ですね。

A: Wow, what a scene!
B: The view from here is the best.

❷ A concert
A：昨日のライブ、最高だったね。
B：ほんと、行ってよかったよ。

A: Yesterday's concert was amazing.
B: It's really a good thing that we went.

❸ An interview
A：優勝おめでとうございます。今のお気持ちは？
B：最高です！

A: Congratulations on your victory. How do you feel?
B: I feel amazing!

❹ Thoughts on a trip
A：温泉旅行は、どうでしたか。
B：最高でしたよ。お風呂はいいし、食事はおいしいし。

A: How was your hot springs trip?
B: It was amazing. The baths were good, and so was the food.

❺ A fun time
A：昨日、誕生日だったんですね。
B：ええ。みんなに祝ってもらって、最高の一日でした。

A: So yesterday was your birthday?
B: Yes. Everyone celebrated it, and it was a wonderful day.

83 最低 *Saitee*
さいてい

The worst

✿ Used to indicate that the content, nature, or situation of something is extremely bad.

POINT
- The antonym of "*saikoo*."
- Often used to evaluate a person's actions or their nature, and in such cases it carries a sense of dissatisfaction or anger.

❶ Someone's personality

A: 野村さんって、何でも人のせいにするよね。
B: ほんと、最低。

A: Nomura-san always blames everything on others.
B: He's really the worst.

❷ Someone's manners

A: あの人、車からたばこ、投げ捨てた。
B: うわー、最低！

A: That person was smoking in their car, then tossed it out the window.
B: Wow, they're the worst!

❸ Someone's personality

A: 人の失敗を笑うなんて、最低。
B: 信じられないよね。

A: How could you laugh at someone's failure? She's the worst.
B: I can't believe it either.

❹ A boss

A: うちの店長はすぐ人に怒鳴るんです。
B: えー、最低。

A: Our manager is quick to yell at people.
B: Wow, that's the worst.

84 さっぱりわからない *Sappari wakaranai*

I don't have a clue

❁ Used to convey a situation of being bewildered due to being completely unable to understand the meaning of something or how something is done.

POINT
➡ *"Sappari ~nai"* means "Not ~ at all."

❶ How to use

A：どうしたの？
B：説明書を読んでも、**さっぱりわからなくて**。

A: What's the matter?
B: I read the instruction manual, but I still don't have a clue.

❷ An article

A：いくら読んでも、**さっぱりわからない**よ。
B：全部英語で書いてあるもんね。

A: I don't have a clue, no matter how many times I read this.
B: Well, it is all written in English, after all.

❸ A girlfriend's thoughts

A：彼女が何を考えているのか、**さっぱりわかりません**。
B：もう一度、しっかり話し合ってみたら？

A: I don't have a clue what my girlfriend is thinking.
B: Why don't you try having a solid talk with her one more time?

❹ Computers

A：パソコンは、**さっぱりわからなくて**。
B：まずはメールの使い方から、一緒に勉強しましょう。

A: I don't have a clue about computers.
B: You should start by learning how to send email. Why don't we study together?

❺ A test

A：**さっぱりわからなかった**から、全部3にマークしたよ。
B：ちょっとぐらいは当たってるかもね。

A: I didn't have a clue, so I just bubbled in 3 for all of the answers.
B: You may have gotten a few of them right.

85 至急、お願いします
Shikyuu onegaishimasu

Please do it as soon as possible; please do it right away

❖ A phrase used when making an emergency request that should be done extremely quickly.

POINT
➡ "*Daishikyuu*" is used when the job needs to be performed even more urgently.
➡ Requires caution when using, as if this phrase is used frequently, it will be devalued and seen as not a credible request.

❶ No parking

A：ここ駐車禁止ですよ。
B：あ、すみません。移動します。
A：**至急、お願いします**ね。

A: Parking is prohibited here.
B: Oh, I'm sorry. I'll move.
A: Please do so right away.

❷ On the phone

A：はい、ＡＢＣタクシーです。
B：すみません、中央病院の玄関前まで**至急お願いします**。

A: Hello, this is ABC Taxi.
B: Excuse me, I need to be taken to the front entrance of Chuo Hospital as soon as possible.

❸ On the phone

A：スミスと申しますが、森さんはいらっしゃいますか。
B：ちょっと席をはずしているんですが、戻ったら電話させましょうか。
A：はい。**至急お願いします**。

A: My name is Smith, is Mori-san available?
B: He is away from his seat right now. Shall I have him call you back once he returns?
A: Yes. Please tell him it's urgent.

❹ On the phone

A：資料をＦＡＸで送ればいいんですね。
B：はい。それで、お忙しいところすみませんが、**至急でお願いします**。

A: Is it okay to send the materials by FAX?
B: Yes. Also, I apologize for asking this when you're busy, but please send them right away.

86 失礼だなあ *Shitsuree da naa*

How rude

❖ Used to express feelings of criticism toward someone's poor attitude or rough treatment toward others.

POINT

➡ "*Shitsuree*" is not only used to describe one's manners, but also more broadly used to speak of someone's general attitude or treatment toward others.

❶ Inside a store

A：あの店員、**失礼だなあ**。
B：どうしたの？
A：今、そこでぶつかったんだけど、何も言わないんだよ。

A: That employee is so rude.
B: What happened?
A: He ran into me just now, but didn't say anything.

❷ Scarier than the president?

A：彼が社長より怖いって言ってたよ。
B：私が!? **失礼だなあ**。そんなこと言ってるんだ。

A: He said you were scarier than the president.
B: Me!? How rude. He was saying things like that?

❸ A bad way to praise someone

A：今日はかわいいね。
B：今日は？ **失礼だなあ**。いつもでしょ！

A: You're looking cute today.
B: Today? How rude. I'm always cute!

Related phrases

❹ 「失礼なこと言わないで」

A：えっ、それ、3個も食べるの！
B：**失礼なこと言わないで**よ。友だちの分よ。

A: Wait, are you eating three of those!?
B: Don't be so rude. These are for my friends.

87 死ぬほど *Shinuhodo*

To death. It almost killed me.

✿ An expression to emphasize degree to a maximum extent.

POINT
➡ It is also used in expressions which are not literally related to "images of [your own] death."
➡ It can be used both in positive and negative senses.
Example: *shinuhodo utsukushii* (extremely beautiful), *shinuhodo suki* (love ~ to death), *shinuhodo kirai* (extreme dislike), *shinuhodo hima* (being bored to death).

---

❶ After the announcement of a test result

A：受かってよかったね。
B：うん！死ぬほど勉強したからね。

A: Good for you for passing the exam.
B: Yes, I studied to death for it.

❷ Possibility

A：ぼくでもオリンピックに出られるかな？
B：死ぬほど努力すれば可能性はあるかもね。

A: Do you think I can participate in the Olympics?
B: Maybe, if you train to death for it.

❸ A funny book

A：これ読んでみて。死ぬほど笑えるから！
B：ほんとに～？

A: Read this. You will kill yourself laughing!
B: Really?

❹ A plan at the end of the year

A：忘年会やる？
B：ごめん、年末は死ぬほど忙しいんだ。

A: Shall we get together for a year-end dinner party?
B: Sorry. I will be extremely busy then.

❺ Accident scene

A：あの時はこっちも慌てたよ。
B：ごめんね。ほんとに死ぬほど痛かったんだよ。

A: I was really panicked.
B: It was so painful. It almost killed me.

88 しばらく様子を見ましょう

Shibaraku yoosu o mimashoo

Let's wait and see

❀ An expression used to suggest waiting and not doing anything to deal with a problem that is occurring and waiting to see how things go.

POINT
▶ Used broadly when wanting to postpone a decision or conclusion.

---

❶ At the hospital

A：昨日から熱が出てしまって…。
B：とりあえず3日分の薬を出しますので、**しばらく様子を見ましょう**。

A: I've had a fever since yesterday...
B: I'll prescribe you three days' worth of medicine, so let's wait and see how things go.

Variations

❷ Buying stock

A：ABCネットの株を買おうと思ってるんだけど。
B：まだ新しい会社だから、**しばらく様子を見たほうがいい**よ。

A: I was thinking of buying stock in ABC Net.
B: It's still a new company, so you should wait and see for a bit longer.

❸ Motivation

A：彼はやる気があるのかなあ。やる気がないなら、やめてもらったほうがいいと思いますよ。
B：ええ…。でも、**もうしばらく様子を見ましょう**。

A: I wonder if he has the motivation to do it. If he doesn't, I think it's better to have him stop.
B: Yes...but let's wait and see for a bit longer.

❹ At the end of its lifespan?

A：この洗濯機も、そろそろだめかもね。買い替える?
B：うん…。**もうちょっと様子を見よう**よ。安い買い物じゃないし。

A: This might be about the end for this washing machine. Do you want to buy a new one to replace it?
B: Well... Let's wait and see for a bit longer. It's not a cheap purchase, after all.

89 冗談じゃない　*Joodan ja nai*

You're joking

❋ It shows the speaker's strong negation that he/she doesn't want to hear such thing even as a joke.

POINT
➡ It shows strong antipathy against a particular decision or remark.

---

❶ Important meeting

A：飛行機が欠航になったみたい。
B：え〜！　冗談じゃないよ、会議があるのに！

A: The flight seems to be canceled.
B: What? You're joking. I should attend the meeting!

❷ Working on holidays

A：部長が土曜日出（ら）れないかって。
B：冗談じゃないよ。毎日遅くまでやってるのに。

A: The manager asked us if we could work on Saturday.
B: You're joking. We have been working till late all the time recently.

❸ Unreliable story

A：彼が言ったことって本当なの？
B：冗談じゃないよ。あんなのデタラメだよ。

A: Was it true what he told us?
B: No way. That's bullshit.

❹ Your hard work comes to nothing

A：先方が契約をキャンセルしたいって。
B：えっ!?　冗談じゃないですよ！　ここまで進めてきたのに。

A: Our client canceled the contract.
B: What? You're joking! We have worked hard for this.

90 知らない *Shiranai*

You're on your own; not my problem

✿ Used to indicate a tough attitude of pushing someone away, stating that you cannot be responsible for what happens to them because they are not heeding your advice or warnings.

POINT
➡ Often used in the form "[expected bad results]+ *temo shiranai yo.*"

❶ A dangerous place

A：そこ、危ないよ！ けがしても**知らない**よ。
B：大丈夫。気をつけてるから。

A: It's dangerous up there! It's not my problem if you get hurt.
B: Don't worry. I'm being careful.

❷ Am I okay?

A：いいから手伝って。
B：失敗しても**知りません**よ。

A: It's fine, just help me.
B: It's not my problem if you fail.

❸ Working too hard

A：そんなに残業ばかりして、倒れても**知りません**よ。
B：うーん、わかってるよ。

A: You're on your own if you collapse from doing all that overtime.
B: Yeah, I know.

❹ Irresponsible

A：大丈夫。どうにかなるって。
B：いいの？ そんな適当で。どうなっても**知らない**よ。

A: Don't worry. It'll work itself out somehow.
B: It's fine? Look at how careless you're being. It's not my problem if something happens to you.

91 素晴らしい *Subarashii*

Wonderful; marvelous; splendid

❀ It is an expression used to praise unconditionally about the state of being significantly better.

POINT
➡ It is used widely for objects of being touched, deeply moved or impressed.

---

❶ Advanced Technology

A: 優れた職人でなければ、ここまでできませんね。

B: ええ、本当に**素晴らしい**です。

A: If he wasn't an outstanding craftsman, he could never come this far.
B: You're right. He is very great.

❷ About a Restaurant

A: この店のサービス、**素晴らしい**ね。

B: うん。また来たいね。

A: The service of this store is impressive.
B: Yes, let's come again.

❸ Good idea

A: これはジムのアイデアなんだ。**素晴らしい**ね。

B: いえいえ。ちょっと思いついただけです。

A: This is your idea, Jim-san? It's fantastic.
B: Thank you, it just popped into my mind.

❹ Basic policies

A: 私は常に、最後まであきらめないで、全力でやりたいんです。

B: その考えは**素晴らしい**と思うよ。

A: I always want to do my best to the end, without giving up.
B: I think that's a great idea.

❺ At a work place

A: 話には聞いてたけど、彼女の仕事ぶりは**素晴らしい**ね。

B: ええ、ほんと頼りになるんです。

A: I've heard about her, and she really does a bully job.
B: Yes, she is very dependable.

92 ずるい *Zurui*

Not fair

✿ An expression used to criticize unfair actions that result in an advantage over others or a similar attitude.

POINT
➡ A term used to criticize others, so it is generally not used with one's superiors.

❶ Submission date

A: 彼、先生に頼んでレポートの期限延ばしてもらったって。
B: えー、**ずるい**。

A: He asked the teacher and got an extension.
B: What? No fair.

❷ Someone else's idea

A: 林さんの企画、本当は山田さんのアイデアだったそうです。
B: 本当ですか。それは**ずるい**ですね。

A: It seems like Hayashi-san's plan was actually Yamada-san's idea.
B: Really? That's no fair.

❸ Borrowing someone's strength

A: 宿題は、友達のを写させてもらうことが多くて。
B: それは**ずるい**よ。

A: I often copy my friends' homework.
B: That's not fair.

❹ Using the internet

A: 面倒だから、ネットで調べちゃった。
B: **ずるい**なあ。自分で考えなよ。

A: It was a pain, so I looked it up on the internet.
B: That's not fair. Figure it out for yourself.

❺ Not saying your own opinion

A: いいよ、みんなと同じ意見で。
B: そういうのは**ずるい**よ。

A: I'm fine with having the same opinion as everyone else.
B: That's not fair.

93 鋭いなあ *Surudoinaa*

How sharp

❁ Used to say that someone's powers of discernment, judgment, etc. are excellent. Used when someone figures out the main point of something quickly.

POINT
➡ "*Kan ga surudoi*" or "*Shiteki ga surudoi*" are also used.

❶ Another reason

A：理由はそれだけじゃないんじゃないですか。
B：さすが、リンダさん。**鋭いなあ**。

A: That must not be the only reason, right?
B: Wow, Linda-san. You really are sharp.

❷ Sharp perception

A：ビルさん、何か隠してない？
B：えっ？　えーっと…。青木さんは勘が**鋭いなあ**。

A: Are you hiding something, Bill-san?
B: Huh? Umm... You're very perceptive, Aoki-san.

❸ Looking at a chart

A：これとこれ、数字が逆だと思います。
B：え？　あ、ほんとだ。**鋭いなあ**。

A: I believe this number and this number are flipped.
B: Huh? Oh, you're right. You're sharp.

❹ The day after drinking

A：昨日飲みすぎたでしょ？
B：あ、ちょっとね…。**鋭いなあ**。

A: You drank too much last night, didn't you?
B: Oh, a bit... You're very sharp.

❺ Comparison

A：同じ記事でも、新聞で読むときとスマホで読むときって、集中力が違う気がするんです。
B：なるほど、その指摘は**鋭いですね**。

A: Even when reading the same article, I feel less focused when reading it on a smartphone as opposed to reading it in a newspaper.
B: I see, that's a very sharp point.

94 全然 Zenzen
ぜんぜん

(Not) at all

❋ It is a short, casual form of *"zenzen ~nai,"* expression used to deny the whole sentence.

POINT

➡ You can convey the message of denial with using only *"zenzen,"* and not along with *"iie."*

---

① Hiking

A：疲れた？
B：いえ、**全然**。

A: Are you tired?
B: No, not at all.

② About an applicant

A：応募してきた人の中でいい人はいましたか。
B：いえ、**全然**でした。

A: Were there any good candidates within the people who applied?
B: No, not one.

③ About a friend

A：ジムはどう？　男性として興味ある？
B：ジム？　**全然**。

A: What about Jim? Any interest in him as a male?
B: Jim? No siree!

④ Simple question

A：貯金はしていますか。
B：いやあ、**全然**です。

A: Are you making any savings?
B: Ah, no, not at all.

⑤ After a match

A：試合はどうでした？
B：もしかしたら勝てるかなと思ったけど、**全然**でした。

A: How was the match?
B: I thought we had some hope of winning, but it was a damn.

95 そういうわけにはいかない

Sooiu wake niwa ikanai

I can't let that happen

❈ **An expression used to deny a proposal by saying "That cannot be done or allowed."**

POINT
➡ Used when making a judgment that something is unacceptable given the current situation or one's own thoughts.

---

❶ At the workplace

A：ここは私がやっとくから、今日はもう帰っていいよ。

B：**そういうわけにはいきません。**

A: I'll do this, so you can go home now.
B: I can't let that happen.

❷ The end is important

A：いいんじゃない、あとは適当でも。

B：**そういうわけにはいかない**よ。仕上げが大切なんだから。

A: What's the matter with not paying so much attention to the rest?
B: I can't let that happen. The way we finish it is important.

❸ Collecting money

A：会費、来週でもいい？

B：だめだめ、**そういうわけにはいかない**よ。

A: Can I pay my membership fee next week?
B: No, no. I can't let that happen.

❹ Something expensive

A：どうぞ、差し上げますよ。

B：**そういうわけにはいきません**よ、こんな高いもの。

A: Here, you can have this.
B: I can't let that happen, not when it's something this expensive.

❺ Hard to turn down

A：行きたくないなら、行かなければいいじゃない。

B：部長の誘いなんだから、**そういうわけにはいかない**よ。

A: If you don't want to go, then just don't go.
B: The department chief invited me, so I can't do that.

110

96 そう思わない? *Soo omowanai?*

Don't you think so? Don't you agree?

✿ **It is used when asking for agreement.**

POINT

➡ When overused, it gives the impression that you are enforcing your ideas by checking for agreement or assent.

---

❶ Using a tool

A：これ、使いにくい。**そう思わない？**
B：確かにね。

A: This is hard to use. Don't you agree?
B: It certainly is.

❷ About a colleague

A：彼は変わってるね。**そう思わない？**
B：そうかなあ。

A: He is odd. Don't you think so?
B: Well, maybe, a bit.

❸ What is needed for successful marriage

A：やっぱり愛でしょう！　**そう思わない？**
B：そうだけど、愛だけでもだめなんだよね。いろいろ揃わないと。

A: It's definitely love! Don't you agree?
B: Yes, but love alone doesn't work. You also need other things.

❹ About university

A：やっぱり、大学出たほうがいいのかなあ。
B：いや、ちゃんと目的がないと大学に行っても意味ないよ。**そう思わない？**

A: Well, I suppose I have to graduate from university.
B: No, unless you have a real goal, being there is meaningless. Don't you think?

111

97 そこをなんとか（お願いします）

Soko o nantoka (onegaishimasu)

Can't you (please) make it work

✿ Used to express feelings of absolutely wanting someone to accept a request when they are displaying a reluctance to do so.

POINT

➡ "*soko*" means "someone's circumstances or situation," while "*nantoka*" means "somehow".

---

❶ Haggling

A：２万５千円？ それは無理ですよ。
B：**そこをなんとか！ お願いします！**

A: 25,000 yen? There's no way.
B: Can't you make it work? Please!

❷ Helping with a move

A：その日は予定があるから無理だよ。
B：**そこをなんとか！ 人手が足りないんだよ。**

A: I can't that day, I already have plans.
B: Can't you make it work!? We don't have enough people.

❸ On the phone

A：日曜日は予約がいっぱいでして…。
B：**そこをなんとかお願いします。** 結婚記念日なんです。

A: I'm busy all Sunday with plans...
B: Can't you please make it work? It is our wedding anniversary.

❹ A job request

A：申し訳ないですが、年内は予定がいっぱいで、全部お断りしているんです。
B：**そこをなんとかお願いします！**

A: I'm sorry, but my schedule is full for the rest of the year, so I've been turning down all offers.
B: Please, can't you make it work?

98 そっか *Sokka*

Is that so

🌸 **A shortened expression of "*soo (nano) ka*".**
  (1) This expression is used when you nod and accept the other person's words for they are.
  (2) This is said when the speaker reaffirms something.

POINT
▶ In case of (2), what the other person said makes the speakers aware of something and they say this expression to themselves. It can be also said when a speaker suddenly recalls or realizes something.

❶ Reason for absence

A：彼女、熱が下がらないんだって。
B：**そっか**。心配だね。

A: I heard her temperature has not come down.
B: Is that so. That's a worrying situation.

❷ Passage of time

A：もうあれから一年だね。
B：**そっか**。早いもんだね。

A: A year has passed since then.
B: Is that so. Time flies.

❸ End in failure

A：すみません。ふじ建設との契約、うまく行きませんでした。
B：**そっか**…。何か新しい手を考えないとね。

A: I'm sorry to say this, but the contract with Fuji Construction didn't go well.
B: Is that so…. We should make a new plan.

❹ Recalling the past

A：**そっか**。もうすぐオリンピックか。
B：ちょっと楽しみだね。

A: Right, we will have the Olympics soon.
B: Looking forward to it.

99 それじゃ *Soreja*

In that case; well then

❀ (1) A phrase said when parting ways with someone.
　(2) A phrase used when beginning or ending one step of work and proceeding to the next step.

POINT
➡ A shortening of "*soredewa.*"

---

❶ When parting

A：また会いましょう。
B：ええ。**それじゃ**。

A: Let's meet again.
B: Yes. In that case.

❷ When parting

A：**それじゃ**あね。
B：うん。**それじゃ**。

A: In that case.
B: Yes, in that case.

❸ A speech

A：じゃ、何か一言お願いします。
B：わかりました。**それじゃ**。

A: Could we ask you to speak a few words?
B: Alright. In that case.

❹ At a home you're visiting

A：遠慮しないで、召し上がってください。
B：はい、**それじゃ**。

A: Don't be reserved, please eat this.
B: Okay, in that case.

100 それでか *Soredeka*

So that's why

✿ Used to express feelings of understanding after learning the basis or reason behind a result or conclusion.

POINT
➡ Can also be said "*~to omottara, soredeka.*"
➡ Said as if speaking to one's self, and primarily among those you are close to.

❶ At the workplace

A: ごめん、のど痛くて声が出ない。
B: ああ、**それでか**。全然しゃべらないからおかしいと思ってたんだよ。

A: Sorry, my throat hurts and I can't talk well.
B: Oh, so that's why. I thought it was strange that you weren't speaking at all.

❷ At the workplace

A: 今日はこれからコンサートに行くんです。
B: **それでか**。なんか急いでるなと思ってたんだよ。

A: I'm going to go to a concert after this today.
B: So that's why. You seemed like you were in a hurry.

❸ A precious pet

A: 彼女、家の猫が死んだんだって。
B: **それでか**。朝からずっと元気なかったもんね。

A: I heard that her housecat died.
B: So that's why. She's seemed down since this morning.

❹ Why it's crowded

A: 今夜、花火大会があるんだって。
B: なるほど。電車が混んでると思ったら、**それでか**。

A: I heard there's a fireworks show tonight.
B: I see. I was wondering why the train was crowded, but that's why.

115

101 それどころじゃない

Soredokoro janai

This isn't the time for that

🌸 Used to communicate that there is something more important than what has just been said. In many cases, it is followed by the phrase "What's important."

POINT
➡ Used in situations that are hurried or confused due to a major matter.

---

❶ At the workplace

A：今日、セールに行かない？
B：ごめん、今忙しくて、**それどころじゃない**んだよ。

A: Do you want to go to the sale today?
B: Sorry, I'm busy today. This isn't the time for me to be doing that.

❷ During lunch

A：今日のお昼、新しくできたピザ屋に行かない？
B：ごめん、今日は**それどころじゃなくて**。また今度行くよ。

A: Do you want to go to the new pizza restaurant for lunch today?
B: Sorry, this isn't the time. I'll go next time.

❸ At the workplace

A：お菓子もらったんだけど、どれがいい？
B：ごめん、今、**それどころじゃなくて**。どれでもいい。

A: We received some snacks, which would you like?
B: Sorry, this isn't the time. Whichever is fine.

❹ A broadcast of an important match

A：ケーキ、食べないの？
B：試合が気になって、**それどころじゃない**んだよ。後で食べる。

A: You're not going to eat any cake?
B: I'm too interested in the match, now isn't the time for that. I'll eat it later.

102 それなりに *Sorenari ni*

In its own way, accordingly, as it is

✿ It is used to express when even though the level or content is not very ideal, yet is in the acceptable range if it's under a certain condition or situation.

POINT
➡ Because it includes a delicate shade of meaning "It's not very ideal…", caution is required when evaluating a person.

---

❶ At a restaurant

A：この店高いなあ。
B：でも、**それなりに**おいしよ。

A: Wow, this store is expensive.
B: Yes, but the quality is in line with the price.

❷ Having a meal with a friend

A：えっ？ 今日はおごってくれるの？
B：まあ、**それなりに**ボーナスも出たから。

A: Really? Are you treating me for a meal?
B: Yep, I got a decent amount of bonus…

❸ With a friend

A：新しい職場はどう？
B：うん、**それなりに**やってるよ。

A: How is your new workplace?
B: Umm, doing so so I guess.

❹ An honor student

A：ケビンさん、成績いいんだって？
B：まあ、**それなりに**ね。

A: Hi Kevin, heard that you have good grades?
B: Yes, well something like that.

❺ Everybody has worries, headaches

A：佐藤さんにも悩みってあるんだね。
B：そりゃあね。**それなりに**はあるよ。

A: So Sato-san has worries, too.
B: That's of course. As it is, I have my worries, too.

117

103 それは痛い *Sore wa itai*

That hurts, that's awful, it's painful

✿ It is an expression used when an incident is a blow to the speaker or the opponent.

POINT

➡ It is used when a painful (hurting) situation is brought about by a shocking incident.

---

❶ A price increase, raise in price

A：食堂のメニューが4月から値上げするんだって。

B：えー、**それは痛い**なあ。

A: The menu in the cafeteria is being raised from April.
B: Oh no, that's a headache.

❷ To lose, to drop

A：買ったばかりのイヤリング、どこかに落としちゃったよ。

B：うわー、**それは痛い**ね。

A: I dropped the earring I just bought somewhere.
B: Wow, it's painful.

❸ Medical expense, doctor's fee

A：うちの犬が入院することになって、治療費が10万円もかかったの。

B：え〜、**それは痛い**ね。

A: Out dog was admitted in the hospital, and we had to shell out 100,000 yen.
B: Really? That hurts.

❹ Not play, don't participate

A：次の試合、カルロスはけがで出られないんだって。

B：うそ！ **それは痛い**なあ。

A: Carlos got hurt, so he's not able to play (participate) in the next game.
B: You're kidding! That's a big blow.

104 それはそうだ *Sore wa soo da*

Of course

❋ Used in reply to someone's statement to indicate that "What you said is correct" or "Of course".

POINT

▶ In speech, "*sore wa*" often becomes "*sorya*."

---

❶ About a concert

A：コンサート、行きたかった？
B：**それはそうだ**よ。こんなチャンス、めったにないんだから。

A: Did you want to go to the concert?
B: Of course I did. There aren't many chances like this one.

❷ Talking about business

A：社長はその話、断ったんだって。
B：**それはそうでしょう**。何もいいことはないからね。

A: I heard the President turned that down.
B: Of course he did. There wasn't a single good thing about it.

❸ Someone's own feelings

A：結局、本人じゃないから、気持ちはわからないよ。
B：**そりゃそうだ**。

A: In the end, we're not her, so we don't know how she feels.
B: Well, of course.

❹ The body is #1

A：病気になったら意味がないよ。体を大切にしないと。
B：**それはそう**なんだけど…。

A: It's pointless if you get sick. You need to stay in good health.
B: Of course, but...

105 それはそうと *Sore wa sooto*

Anyway; putting that aside; moving on

❋ An expression used when moving away from one topic of conversation to another.

POINT
➡ A shortening of *"sore wa soo toshite."*
➡ *"Sore wa sateoki"* is used to mean roughly the same thing in a more formal way. In this case, *"sate + oki"* means *"sonoyoo ni shite + oite."*

❶ With friends

A：新しい職場はどう？
B：順調だよ。**それはそうと**、来月ハワイに行くんだけど、おすすめの場所、ない？

A: How is your new workplace?
B: It's fine. Anyway, I'm going to be going to Hawaii next month. Do you have any places you'd suggest?

❷ At work

A：昨日はごちそうさまでした。奥様の料理最高でした！
B：伝えておくよ。**それはそうと**、森さんのケータイの番号、知ってる？

A: Thank you for the meal yesterday. Your wife's cooking was amazing!
B: I'll let her know. Anyway, do you know Mori-san's cell phone number?

❸ At work

A：今日も暑いですね。
B：ええ。いやになりますよ。…あ、**それはそうと**、最近、引っ越したそうですね。

A: It's hot today too.
B: Yes, annoyingly so. …Oh, putting that aside, I heard you moved recently.

❹ After a meeting

A：じゃ、この件は次回また話しましょう。**それはそうと**、皆さんはもう夏休みの予定は立てましたか。
B：私はまだです。

A: Then let's talk about this next time. Moving on, do you all have plans for summer break already?
B: Not yet for me.

106 それはないよ *Sore wa nai yo*

No way; unreasonable

❉ Expresses dissatisfaction or disappointment with some unreasonable statement or unfair treatment.

POINT
➡ Used when protesting to someone or complaining to oneself.
➡ It has several variations, including "sorya nai yo, "*sore wa nai deshoo*," and "*sore wa nai daroo*."

❶ Too late

A：ビルさん、来るの遅すぎ。もう料理残ってないよ。
B：え〜！ それはないよ。

A: Bill, you're too late. There's no food left.
B: What? No way!

❷ Before a test

A：明日の漢字のテスト、100問もあるんだって。
B：え〜！ それはないよ。無理だよ。

A: I heard the kanji test tomorrow is going to have 100 questions.
B: What? No way. That's excessive.

Variations

❸ Transportation expenses

A：交通費は自己負担だって。
B：え〜！ それはないんじゃない？

A: They say we have to pay for transportation ourselves.
B: What? That's unreasonable.

❹ Cancellation

A：イベント、中止だって。
B：ここまで準備したのに？ それはないでしょ！

A: I heard the event is canceled.
B: When we've gotten this far with preparations? No way!

107 それはよかった *Sore wa yokatta*

That's great

❁ Used to convey that you are also happy because something joyous happened to someone else.

POINT
➡ The basic form of this is expressing *"yokatta"* in the past tense.
➡ In the case of *"Sore wa ii desu ne."*, the phrase becomes one evaluating someone's proposal or plan.

❶ At an airport

A：スーツケース、無事に見つかりました。
B：見つかった？ **それはよかった**ですね。

A: We found the suitcase without any problems.
B: You found it? That's good to hear.

❷ Passing

A：やっと合格したよ。
B：**それはよかった**ですね。

A: I finally passed.
B: That's good to hear.

❸ At a hospital

A：検査の結果、特に異常はありませんでした。
B：**それはよかった**ですね。

A: There was nothing unusual in the test results.
B: That's good to hear.

❹ Notice of employment

A：おかげさまで就職先が決まりました。
B：**それはよかった**ですね。じゃ、お仕事頑張ってくださいね。

A: I found work thanks to you.
B: That's good to hear. Good luck at your job, now.

❺ Near from home

A：新しい職場は家からも近いんです。
B：へー、**それはよかった**じゃない。

A: My new workplace is close to my home.
B: Oh, that's good to hear.

108 それほどでもないです

Sorehodo demo nai desu

Not really; it's nothing, really

✿ Used to convey that something is not to the degree that someone says, while also showing one's feelings of modesty.

POINT
➡ Used when someone praises you.
➡ Said in earnest in some situations, while said in other situations to stress one's attitude of modesty.

❶ At a party

A：この料理、全部森さんが作ったんですか。すごい！
B：いやあ、**それほどでもないです**よ。

A: Did you make this entire meal yourself, Mori-san? That's amazing!
B: Oh, it's nothing really.

❷ At a shop

A：すごい高級ブランドですね。高かったんでしょう？
B：いや、これは**それほどでもなかったんです**よ。

A: This is a very luxurious brand. It must have been expensive, right?
B: Oh, not really.

❸ Language skill

A：森さんって、英語ペラペラだそうですね。
B：いやあ、**それほどでもないです**よ。日常会話程度ですよ。

A: Mori-san, you seem like you're fluent in English.
B: Oh, not really. I can only manage regular conversations.

❹ Commute time

A：毎日２時間もかけて通学してるの？　大変だね。
B：うん…。でも、慣れれば**それほどでもない**よ。

A: You spend two hours traveling to school each day? That must be difficult.
B: Well… It's not so bad once you get used to it.

❺ Late for the appointment

A：遅れてすみません。だいぶ待ったんじゃないですか。
B：いや、**それほどでもない**よ。

A: I'm sorry for being late. You must have waited for a while.
B: Oh, not that long.

123

109 それを聞いて安心した

Sore o kiite anshin shita

I'm relieved to hear that

✿ Used to express feelings of relief when one hears something said by someone else.

POINT

➡ "Sore o kiite ~." is an expression used when one's feelings change as the result of something said by another person. "Ureshii" or "odoroita" can also be used in this situation.

❶ Good news

A：明日の授業、休講だって。
B：ほんと？ それを聞いて安心したよ。レポート、まだ終わってないんだ。

A: I heard that class is canceled tomorrow.
B: Really? I'm relieved to hear that. I'm not done with my report yet.

❷ A typhoon is coming

A：台風、こっちには来ないんだって。
B：ほんと？ それを聞いて安心したよ。週末、引っ越しだから。

A: I heard that the typhoon won't be coming this way.
B: Really? I'm relieved to hear that. I'm moving this weekend.

❸ About a business trip

A：来週のアメリカ出張、通訳が一緒に行くらしいですよ。
B：それを聞いて安心しました。英語苦手なんですよ。

A: It sounds like an interpreter will be accompanying next week's business trip to America.
B: I'm glad to hear that. I'm no good at English.

❹ Way of payment

A：支払いは分割でもいいそうですよ。
B：それを聞いて安心した。10万円って、けっこう大金だからね。

A: It seems like you can pay in installments, too.
B: I'm glad to hear that. 100,000 yen is quite a large sum.

Related phrases

❺ 「それを聞いてほっとした」

A：彼女、全然怒ってなかったよ。
B：ほんと？ それを聞いてほっとしたよ。ずっと気になってたから。

A: She didn't get mad at all.
B: Really? I'm glad to hear that. I was always so worried.

110 そんな感じです *Sonna kanji desu*

Something like that

❋ **It is an expression used when communicating roughly about certain contents and situations.**

POINT
▶ It is used when roughly explaining (*konna kanji*), agreeing to (*sonna kanji*), or inquiring (*donna kanji?*) about something.

---

❶ After an explanation

A：…休みの日は大体**そんな感じです**。
B：そうですか。結構忙しいんですね。

A: ….I sort of spend my holidays like that.
B: I see. You seem to be very busy.

❷ A basic question

A：ニューヨークの生活って**どんな感じ？**
B：東京とかなり似てるよ。

A: How is life in New York?
B: Oh, it's very similar to life in Tokyo.

❸ A simple question

A：寮の部屋ってどんな感じ？
B：〈写真を見せながら〉**こんな感じ**だよ。

A: What is the dorm room like?
B: [while showing a picture] It's like this.

❹ Reflect on, think something over

A：最近、全然家族に電話できてないなあ。
B：ああ、私も**そんな感じ**。

A: Oh boy, I'm not able to call my family at all recently.
B: Yep, me too.

111 そんなに（あんまり）急かさないで

Sonna ni (anmari) sekasanaide

Don't rush me so much

❖ Used to express dissatisfaction or antipathy toward someone rushing you.

POINT
▶▶ "*Sekasu*" means to try to hurry someone's actions through words or attitude.

❶ Preparing for a meal

A：食器、まだ出してないの？　早く出してよ。
B：**そんなに急かさないで**よ。今やろうと思ってたんだから。

A: The table isn't set yet? Hurry up and do it.
B: Don't rush me so much. I was going to do it just now.

❷ At a restaurant

A：まだ決まらないの？
B：**そんなに急かさないで**よ。いろいろあって迷うんだから。

A: You still haven't decided?
B: Don't rush me so much. There's so much here I don't know what to get.

❸ Before leaving

A：ねえ、準備できた？　行ける？
B：**あんまり急かさないで**よ。忘れ物したら後で困るんだから。

A: Hey, are you ready? Can you go?
B: Don't rush me so much. It'll be a problem later if I forget something.

❹ Tourism

A：もうちょっと早く歩けない？
B：なんで？　ゆっくり見たいんだから、**あんまり急かさないで**よ。

A: Can you walk a little faster?
B: Why? I want to take my time to see this, so don't rush me so much.

112 そんなばかな *Sonna baka na*

Such nonsense; how can that be?

Abbreviated form of "*Sonna bakana koto ga aru hazuganai* (Something so ridiculous is not expected to exist)". Expresses negative feelings, surprise, and disappointment when something unreasonable or seemingly impossible has actually happened.

POINT
➤ This is a comment said to oneself. It is not meant as an insult to someone.

❶ At a shop

A: そのお品物は販売中止になりました。
B: え、**そんなばかな**。人気あったのに。

A: That product has been discontinued.
B: How can that be? It was popular.

❷ Risigning

A: 残念ですが、田中さんが今月で退社することになりました。
B: えー、**そんなばかな**。田中さんがいないと困るよ。

A: Unfortunately, Tanaka-san is leaving the company this month.
B: No way. It will be hard to get by without Tanaka-san.

❸ About the favorite team

A: ライオンズ、負けちゃったよ。
B: えー、**そんなばかな**！ 相手はそんなに強くないじゃない。

A: The Lions lost the game.
B: How could they have lost? The other team isn't all that good.

❹ A popular shop

A: この店が人気ナンバーワン！？ **そんなばかな**！
B: この雑誌、いいかげんなんだよ。

A: This is the most popular shop? How could that be true?
B: This magazine is not very accurate.

113 そんなはずはない *Sonnna hazu wa nai*

It can't be so

❀ Used to confidently deny what the other person is saying.

POINT
➡ It may also express surprise or unwillingness to accept that something is a fact.

❶ Can't find

A：だめ。どこ探してもなかった。
B：**そんなはずはない**よ。外に出てないんだから、絶対家の中にあるはず。

A: It's no good. It wasn't anywhere I looked.
B: It can't be lost. I haven't gone out, so it's definitely in the house.

❷ Surprising couple

A：ビルとスーザンが結婚するんだって。
B：**そんなはずはない**よ。あの二人じゃ、全然合わないよ。

A: I heard Bill and Susan are getting married.
B: That can't be. Those two would be completely wrong for each other.

❸ Family budget

A：彼女も経済的に苦しいって。
B：**そんなはずはない**よ。共働きでかなり余裕があるはずだよ。

A: She said she's in financial difficulty.
B: That can't be. Both she and her husband work, so they should have plenty.

❹ Budget

A：3万円用意すれば足りるはず。
B：**そんなはずないよ**。往復の交通費だけで2万円するんだから。

A: It should be enough if we set aside 30,000 yen.
B: I don't think so. Just the round-trip ticket alone costs 20,000 yen.

114 そんな日もあるよ

Sonna hi mo aru yo

There are days like that

🌸 An expression used to cheer people on by saying "There are good days and bad days in life" to someone who has experienced something unfortunate or for whom things are not going well.

POINT
➡ After actually witnessing someone's day, *"Kooiu hi mo aru yo."* is used, while *"Sonna hi mo aru yo."* is used when only hearing about their day.

---

❶ No energy

A：なんか全然元気出なくて…。
B：ま、そんな日もあるよ。天気もよくないしね。

A: For some reason, I feel completely unenergetic...
B: Well, there are days like that. The weather isn't good, either.

❷ Apologizing for failures

A：失敗ばかりして、今日は本当に申し訳ありませんでした。
B：まあ、気にしないで。そんな日もあるよ。

A: I've done nothing but fail, I'm truly sorry about today.
B: Well, don't worry about it. There are days like that.

❸ Sports

A：今日は全然だめだったね。
B：たまにはそんな日もあるよ。しょうがない。

A: Today was no good at all.
B: There are sometimes days like that. There's nothing you can do about it.

Variations -

❹ An unlucky day

A：今日はほんとについてない。コンタクトレンズはなくすし、上司には怒られるし。
B：まあ、そういう日もあるよ。元気出して。

A: I'm really unlucky today. Not only did I lose my contact lenses, my boss got mad at me.
B: Well, there are sometimes days like that. Cheer up.

115 そんなもんだよ

Sonnamon da yo

That's how it is

❁ Used to express feelings of resignation by stating one must simply accept reality when something dissatisfying has happened.

POINT

➡ Often used together with terms such as *"jinsee wa," "ningen wa"* and *"genjitsu wa."*

❶ Not like he used to be

A: 彼も出世して変わったな。付き合いにくくなったよ。

B: 人間なんて、**そんなもんだよ**。

A: He's changed after he was promoted. It's harder to be with him.
B: That's how people are.

❷ Once I became an adult...

A: 大人になったら何でも自由にできると思ってたけど、そうでもないな。

B: 現実は**そんなもんだよ**。

A: I thought I'd be able to do anything I wanted once I became an adult, but that wasn't the case.
B: That's how reality is.

Related phrases

❸ 「そういうもんだよ」

A: かわいい子には必ず彼氏がいるんだよね。

B: **そういうもんだよ**。あ～あ、彼女ほしいなあ。

A: Cute girls always have boyfriends.
B: That's how it is. Oh, I wish I had a girlfriend.

❹ 「そういうもんだよ」

A: 〈抽選の後で〉ハワイ旅行、ちょっと期待したんだけどなあ。ティッシュとタオルか…。

B: ま、**そういうもんだよ**。

A: [After a lottery] I was hoping I would win the trip to Hawaii. But I just got tissues and a towel...
B: Well, that's how it is.

116 大したことない

Taishitakotonai

It's nothing special; it's no big deal

❀ Used to express that something is not that major.

POINT
➡ Can be used to evaluate something both positively or negatively.

❶ Watching a sports match

A：今日の相手は強いの？
B：いや、大したことないよ。

A: Is the other team strong today?
B: No, they're nothing special.

❷ A new film

A：昨日の映画、どうだった？
B：評判いいらしいけど、大したことなかったよ。

A: How was the movie yesterday?
B: It apparently has good reviews, but it was nothing special.

❸ Injury

A：けがしたって聞いたけど、大丈夫？
B：大したことないよ。ちょっとぶつけただけだから。

A: I heard you got hurt, are you okay?
B: It's no big deal. I just bumped into something.

❹ A gift

A：え？ こんな高価なもの、もらっていいんですか。
B：大したことないですよ。よかったら使ってください。

A: What? Is it really okay for me to receive something this expensive?
B: It's no big deal. Use it if you like it.

❺ Crowded?

A：新幹線、混んでたんじゃない？
B：いえ、大したことなかったですよ。

A: Wasn't the shinkansen crowded?
B: No, it was no big deal.

131

117 大したもんだ *Taishita monda*

Impressive; a big deal

❁ Used to express one's admiration for a high level of skill or technique.

POINT
➡ When speaking polite, use *"Taishita mono desu (ne)."*

---

❶ Preparing for a party

A: クッキーも焼いたよ。

B: へえ。これ、全部自分で作ったんだ。**大したもんだ**なあ。

A: I baked cookies, too.

B: Wow. You made all of these yourself? That's impressive.

❷ Boom

A: ここは5年前まで何もなかったんです。

B: へえ。たった5年でこんなに発展したんだ。**大したもんだ**なあ。

A: There wasn't anything here until five years ago.

B: Wow. All of this development in just five years. That's impressive.

❸ Brilliant achievement

A: リンダさん、日本語の勉強を始めて1年でN1に合格したんだって。

B: へえ、**大したもんだ**ね。

A: I heard that Linda-san passed the N1 just a year after she began studying Japanese.

B: Wow, that's impressive.

❹ Good singer?

A: 森さんって、歌が上手なんでしょ？ 聞いたことある？

B: あるよ。一回一緒にカラオケに行ったことがあるけど、**大したもんだった**よ。

A: Mori-san is a good singer, right? Have you heard her before?

B: I have. I went to sing karaoke with her before, and she was impressive.

118 耐えられない *Taerarenai*

Can't bear

✿ A phrase used in a difficult situation to express that it is very painful and that one cannot bear it any longer.

POINT
➡ A negation of the potential form of "*taeru*," or "*taerareru*."

❶ A difficult workplace

A: もう、こんな会社耐えられないよ。
B: じゃ、さっさとやめたほうがいいよ。

A: I can't bear this company any longer.
B: Then you should go ahead and quit.

❷ Humiliation

A: あんな男にばかにされるなんて、耐えられないよ。
B: そうだね。

A: I can't bear being made a fool of by that man.
B: You're right

❸ Parting ways with a loved one

A: 半年も彼に会えないなんて、耐えられない。
B: 半年は長いよね。

A: I can't bear not being able to see him for half a year.
B: Half a year is long.

❹ Places of living

A: こういうところに住むのって、どう？
B: 私にはちょっと耐えられないな。

A: What do you think about living in a place like this?
B: I don't think I'd really be able to bear it.

❺ Harsh heat

A: だめだ。この暑さはちょっと耐えられない。
B: うん。どこかお店に入ろう。

A: I can't do it. This heat is too much for me to bear.
B: Yeah. Let's go into a store somewhere.

133

119 だから言ったのに *Dakara itta noni*

I told you, that's what I said, what did I tell you?

✿ It is used to express an accusation or disappointment against one's failure, because they had failed to listen to your advice, or had not paid attention to it.

POINT

➡ It is often used often when your caution and advice was ignored or taken lightly.

---

❶ Hangover

A：朝から頭が痛いよ。
B：だから言ったのに。飲みすぎないようにって。

A: I have a splitting headache from morning.
B: That's why I told you, not to drink too much.

❷ Cause for catching a cold

A：ああ…、風邪ひいたみたい。
B：だから言ったのに。ちゃんと暖かくしないとだめだって。

A: Ohhh.... It seems like I caught a cold.
B: See? I told you you needed to keep warm.

❸ Important to take steps

A：部長にいきなり怒られちゃったよ。
B：だから言ったのに。まず部長に相談したほうがいいって。

A: I was scolded by my manager out of the blue sky.
B: I told you so! That you should consult your manager first.

Related phrases -

❹「だから言ったでしょ」

A：まさか原さんが怒るとは思わなかったよ。
B：だから言ったでしょ。彼女は結構難しいんだって。

A: I never dreamed that Hara-san would get angry.
B: What did I tell you? She is very difficult.

134

120 だよね *Da yo ne*

I knew it. I thought so.

❖ This is a shortened expression of *"soo da yo ne, soo desu yo ne."* It is used to agree with the other speaker.

POINT

➡ This is an informal expression. You had better not use this with someone you meet for the first time.

---

❶ Not available tonight

A：ごめん、今夜は予定があって。
B：**だよね**。急に誘ってごめん。

A: I'm sorry, but I have an appointment tonight.
B: I thought so. It was my fault to invite you without notice.

❷ At the office

A：悪いけど、今日は残業になる。
B：**ですよね**。早く終わるかなって、ちょっと期待したんですけど。

A: I'm afraid we will have to work overtime.
B: I knew it. I kind of expected we might be able to finish up early.

❸ At the office

A：リサさんなら、もう帰ったよ。
B：**だよね**。そうかなとは思ったんだけど。

A: Lisa has already gone back home.
B: I knew it. Actually, I thought she might.

❹ Submission of an application

A：すみませんが、もう受け付けは終了したんです。
B：**ですよね**。失礼しました。

A: I'm sorry to say this, but the submission date has passed.
B: I knew it. Sorry.

135

121 頼りにしてます

Tayori ni shitemasu

Counting on you, rely on you, depend on you

❋ It is used to express the feeling of expectation that the other person's cooperation or work would be a great help or strength for you.

POINT

➡ It includes the feeling of expectation or reliance along with trust and hope towards the other person.

❶ Help moving

A：引っ越し手伝うから、何でも言って。
B：頼りにしてます。

A: I'll help with your moving, so let me know if you need any help.
B: You promised.

❷ Everyone's hope

A：頑張りますので、これからもよろしくお願いします。
B：みんな頼りにしてますよ。

A: I'll do my best, and I appreciate your continuous support.
B: We're expecting your work.

❸ Linguistic Ability

A：中国語がわかるのはワンさんだけだから、頼りにしてますよ。
B：そうか。私だけか。

A: Mr. Wan is the only one that understands Chinese, so we are counting on you.
B: I see, it's only me.

❹ Expert

A：もう6、7年この仕事をしています。
B：じゃ、ベテランですね。頼りにしてます。

A: I've been on this job for 6~7 years already.
B: Then you're an expert. We are relying on you.

❺ Reliable helper

A：しょうがないなあ。じゃ、今回は手伝うよ。
B：やった！ 頼りにしてるよ。

A: All right, I'll help you only for this one time.
B: Hurray! I'm depending on you.

122 違う *Chigau*

No; that's wrong

- 1: An expression used to indicate that something someone has said is wrong.
- 2: Used to express that something under consideration is different from how you imagined it.

POINT
➡ A clear and straightforward declaration.

---

❶ In the way

A：これ、ここに置いたの、ビルさん？
B：**違います**。ぼくじゃないです。

A: Did you put this here, Bill-san?
B: No. It wasn't me.

❷ Next week's plans

A：来週、旅行に行くんだっけ？
B：**違う**よ。出張だよ。

A: So you're going on a vacation next week?
B: That's wrong. It's a business trip.

❸ How it should be done

A：全員無料にすれば公平なんじゃない？
B：それは**違う**と思う。

A: Wouldn't it be fair if it was free for everyone?
B: I think that's wrong.

❹ His opinion

A：トニーは税金を上げるのに反対なんでしょ？
B：**違います**。税金で問題を解決するのが反対なんです。

A: Tony, you're against raising taxes, right?
B: That's wrong. I'm against solving problems using tax money.

❺ A design proposal

A：どう、このデザイン？
B：うーん、なんか**違う**なあ。

A: What do you think about this design?
B: Hm, something seems wrong about it.

123 力が出ない *Chikara ga denai*

Have no strength; have no motivation

✿ Loss of energy from physical or emotional disorder.

POINT
➡ There are "physical reasons" from hunger, sickness and tiredness, and "emotional reasons" from painful events or worries.

❶ Eating habits

A：ぼくは朝食は食べないんです。
B：私はだめ。朝、食べないと**力が出ない**。

A: I don't eat breakfast.
B: Not me. If I don't eat breakfast, then I feel weak.

❷ Meal

A：あんまりお腹空いてないから、いいよ。
B：だめだよ、ちゃんと食べないと。**力出ない**よ。

A: It's ok, I don't feel very hungry.
B: No, you have to eat right, or you won't have any strength.

❸ A shocking incident

A：だめだ。全然**力が出ない**。
B：そんなにショックだったんだ。

A: No, I can't do it. I haven't the strength.
B: Must have been very shocking.

❹ Lack of sleep

A：どうも**力が出ない**。寝不足のせいかなあ。
B：ああ、きっとそうだよ。

A: I'm not strong enough. Maybe it's from lack of sleep.
B: Yea, it must be.

124 調子はどう? *Chooshi wa doo?*

How are you doing? How is it coming along?

❃ **It is an expression used to inquire how things are coming along, or about the condition.**

POINT
➡ It is an expression used to inquire especially whether it's "good or bad."
➡ The subject varies from physical condition, work, life and machine etc.

❶ Injuries

A：足の**調子はどう**ですか。
B：だいぶよくなりました。

A: How is your leg?
B: It's so much better, thank you.

❷ At workplace

A：**調子はどう**？
B：いやあ、忙しいですよ。

A: How are you coming along?
B: Phew, I'm very busy.

❸ Before the match or game

A：**調子はどう**ですか。
B：すごくいいですよ。早く試合がしたいです。

A: How is your condition?
B: Very well, thank you. I can't wait to play.

❹ About the copy machine

A：修理した後、**調子はどう**？
B：今のところ、問題ないです。

A: How is the machine after it was fixed?
B: No problem so far.

❺ With a friend

A：久しぶり。最近、**調子はどう**？
B：うん。まあ、元気にやってるよ。そっちは？

A: Hi, long time no see. How have you been?
B: Doing so so. And you?

125 冷たいなあ *Tsumetai naa*

You're cold; You're nasty

❀ It is an expression used to accuse someone who couldn't care less about others, or taking and showing an unfriendly attitude toward others.

POINT
➡ This is said about the cold attitude of not only the speaker, but also towards any person or an animal.

❶ At the office

A：じゃ、先に帰るね。
B：え、手伝ってくれないの？ 冷たいなあ。

A: Ok, I'm off.
B: What, you're not helping us? You're cold.

❷ To be disappointed with

A：困ってたのに、誰も助けてくれなかったんだよ。
B：えー、冷たいね。

A: I was in trouble, but nobody gave me a hand.
B: What a bummer!

❸ On the phone

A：なにか用？ あんまり時間ないんだけど。
B：別に用はないけど…。なんか冷たいなあ。

A: What's up? Sorry, I don't have much time…
B: Well, nothing special… but why do you cut coldly?

❹ About a colleague

A：彼女、森さんに冷たくない？
B：なんか気に入らないんだろうね。

A: Doesn't she give Mori-san the cold shoulder?
B: There must be something she doesn't like about her.

126 つらい *Tsurai*

Tough; difficult; rough

❁ To feel physical or mental burden or pain, or to feel like you don't want to be doing something.

POINT

➡ "*Tsurai*" originally meant "So difficult or painful that it's unbearable", but it is also used in less serious situations.

❶ Expenses

A: 送料が1000円かかるんだって。
B: それはちょっと**つらい**ね。

A: It seems like shipping will be 1,000 yen.
B: That's a little rough.

❷ Work conditions

A: この会社、お金はいいんだけど、転勤がすごく多いみたい。
B: それはちょっと**つらい**なあ。

A: The money is good at this company, but there seem to be a lot of transfers.
B: That might be a little tough.

❸ The day before a business trip

A: 明日、一日中雨だって。
B: うそ。荷物が多いから、ちょっと**つらい**なあ。

A: It's supposed to rain all day tomorrow.
B: No way. I have a lot of luggage, so that's going to be tough.

❹ Can't go together

A: 結局、一緒には行ってくれないんだよね。
B: そう言われると**つらい**んだけど…。

A: So in the end, you won't be going with me.
B: It's tough when you put it that way, but...

127 同感です *Dookan desu*
どうかん

I agree

🌸 Used to show agreement or sympathy with someone's opinion, as if to say "I think so too" or "I feel the same way too."

POINT
➡ "*(Watashi mo) dookan (desu).*" is the base form.

---

❶ Social problems

A：日本は経済優先で、こういう人たちに甘すぎると思います。
B：私も同感です。

A: Japan puts its economy first and is too easy on these kinds of people, I think.
B: I agree.

❷ While walking outside

A：この辺、もっと緑を増やしてほしいなあ。
B：同感です。

A: I wish they would make this area more green.
B: I agree.

❸ A team you support

A：この監督じゃ、チームは強くならないよ。
B：全く同感。

A: The team's never going to get better with this manager.
B: I completely agree with you.

❹ At the workplace

A：前のデザインのほうがよかったな。
B：同感。変える必要なかったよ。

A: I liked the old design better.
B: I agree. There was no need to change it.

❺ While watching TV

A：私もあの人の言うことに同感。正しいと思う。
B：ぼくはちょっと違うんだよね。

A: I agree with what that person is saying. I think she's right.
B: I see things a little differently.

128 同情するよ *Doojoo suru yo*

I sympathize

❋ To imagine the painful feelings held by another as if they were your own.

POINT
➤ As this includes a feeling of pity, it is not used with those superior to you.

---

① Noise problem

A：それは辛いね。同情するよ。
B：ええ。だから、もう、早く引っ越したくて。

A: That sounds tough. I sympathize with you.
B: Yes. And that's why I want to move soon.

② Watching the news

A：かわいそうだな、この人たち。同情するよ。
B：ほんとだね。

A: Those poor people. I sympathize with them.
B: Yes, really.

③ After a trip overseas

A：カメラ、盗まれたんだって？ 同情するよ。ぼくも経験あるから。
B：はい…。もう、ショックで…。

A: I heard your camera was stolen? I sympathize with you. It happened to me once too.
B: Yes… It's such a shock to me…

④ Switching seats

A：えっ、部長の目の前の席になったの!? 同情するよ。
B：まあ、しょうがないです。

A: What? You were moved to the seat in front of the department chief? I sympathize.
B: Well, what can you do.

⑤ An unlucky coworker

A：彼には同情するよ。
B：ほんと、ついてないね。

A: I sympathize with him.
B: He really is unlucky.

129 どうってことない *Doottekoto nai*

No big deal. Nothing to worry about.

✿ This shows that there is nothing to be concerned about.

POINT
- A shortened expression of "*doo to iu koto wa nai.*"
- It can be also said "*nan to iu koto mo nai*", "*nante koto nai*", etc.

---

❶ Slight injury

A：けが、大丈夫ですか。
B：ああ。これぐらい、**どうってことない**よ。

A: Is your injury all right?
B: Yes, it's nothing to worry about.

❷ Having a fever

A：熱があるんじゃないですか。顔が赤いですよ。
B：ちょっとね。でも、**どうってことない**よ。

A: You might have a fever. You have a red face.
B: Only a little bit. But it's no big deal.

❸ Distance to a destination

A：駅まで歩いて行くんですか。ちょっと遠くないですか。
B：**どうってことない**ですよ。

A: Are you walking to the station? Isn't it a bit far?
B: No big deal.

❹ The opposition (sport)

A：今度の相手、強そうなんです。
B：**どうってことない**よ。大丈夫、絶対勝てるから。

A: The opposition for the next match looks strong.
B: Nothing to worry about. You'll be all right. You can win.

❺ A challenge

A：難しそう〜。私なんかにできるんでしょうか。
B：いや、これぐらい別に**どうってことない**ですよ。

A: Looks difficult. Do you think I can make it?
B: Yes, there is nothing to worry about.

130 どうでもいい *Doo demo ii*

Don't care a bit, don't give a damn, whatever

✿ It is used to express there is no meaning to, or is not an subject of some interest to myself of today or the present situation.

POINT
➡ Sometimes it simply means "noting in particular, anything is ok", so you need to distinguish it from "having no interest, not important at all".

❶ Ready to leave or go out

A：傘、どっちがいいかな？
B：そんなの**どうでもいい**から急いで！

A: Which umbrella do you prefer?
B: It doesn't matter, just hurry up!

❷ Making a reservation at a hotel

A：部屋の広さは**どうでもいい**から、とにかく駅から近いほうがいい。
B：わかりました。じゃ、それで予約しておきますね。

A: As long as it's close to the station, the size of the room doesn't matter.
B: All right. I'll reserve a room according to that.

❸ About financial condition, management situation

A：あの会社、経営厳しいらしいよ。
B：ずっと前に辞めた会社だし、もう**どうでもいい**よ。

A: The management situation of that company seems to be in a crisis.
B: I quit that company a long time ago, so it makes no difference to me.

❹ About a rumor being spread, get wind of, gossip about

A：私は別に**どうでもいい**。
B：すごいね。私は気になっちゃう。

A: Who cares? It's none of my business.
B: Wow! It sure matters a lot to me.

131 どうなってる? *Doonatteru?*

What's going on?; What's this all about?; What's happening?

✿ (1) It is an expression used to find out what the present status is like on a thing or a situation.
(2) It is an expression used to raise questions and show disappointments towards the present situation.

POINT
➡ If you emphasize or raise the tone like "What's the deal?", "What in the hell is going on?", it will mean you're accusing or protesting against it.

---

❶ At the workplace

A: 例のあれ、**どうなってる？**
B: はい、もうすぐできます。

A: What's the situation on that matter?
B: Oh, it will be done soon.

❷ At a restaurant

A: もう１時間も待ってるんですけど。**どうなってるんですか**。
B: すみません。すぐにお持ちします。

A: I've already been waiting for an hour. What is going on?
B: I'm very sorry. I'll serve it right away.

❸ On operating a machine

A: 全然動かない。これ、**どうなってるの？**
B: ここを押せばいいんだよ。

A: What's wrong with this? It doesn't move at all.
B: You just need to press here.

Variations -

❹ About the future

A: 2030年か…。その頃、地球は**どうなってるんだろうね**。
B: そうだね。

A: Year 2030? I wonder what the earth will be like then.
B: Ummm, me too.

132 どうやって? *Dooyatte*

How?

✿ It is an expression used to inquire means, methods or ways of doing things.

POINT
➡ It is used to express surprises or praise at times, too.

---

① How to make

A：えっ!? それ自分で作ったの!? **どうやって？**
B：今度教えるよ。

A: Wow!? Did you make that all by yourself!? How?
B: I'll teach you next time.

② How to get, obtain it

A：見て。やっと買えた。
B：それ、今どこにも売ってないのに！ **どうやって？**

A: Look! I finally got this.
B: They don't sell that anymore now! How in the world did you get it?

Variations -

③ How to eat

A：これ、**どうやって**食べるんですか？
B：手で持って食べるんだよ。

A: Well, how do you eat this?
B: You just pick it with your hand and eat it.

④ How to apply

A：このサービスは**どうやって**申し込むんですか。
B：ABCのホームページで手続きをするんだよ。

A: How am I supposed to apply for this service?
B: You apply from the ABC homepage.

133 道理で Doori de

That makes sense

✿ Used to express feelings of understanding after learning about a reason or situation that explains something you had wondered about.

POINT

➡ The forms "Doori de ~ hazu da." "Doori de ~ to omotta." are also frequently used.

❶ Why someone couldn't be contacted

A: 彼女、先週からタイに旅行に行ってますよ。
B: 道理で。全然、連絡がつかなかったんですよ。

A: She's been on vacation in Thailand since last week.
B: That makes sense. I hadn't been able to get in contact with her at all.

❷ Why she doesn't speak ill of him

A: あの二人は付き合ってるんですよ。
B: 道理で。彼女、彼のこと、悪く言わないから。

A: Those two are going out.
B: That makes sense. She never says anything bad about him.

❸ Why there's traffic

A: 今日はお祭りがあるみたい。
B: 道理で。この道は普段、そんなに混んでないからね。

A: It seems like there's a festival today.
B: That makes sense. This street usually isn't that crowded.

❹ Why someone's smiling

A: 課長、子どもが生まれたんだって。
B: 道理で。なんか、にこにこしてるなあって思ってた。

A: The section chief's child was just born.
B: That makes sense. He seemed like he was smiling a lot.

134 特(とく)にない／特(とく)には

Tokuni nai / Tokuniwa

Not really; nothing in particular

❀ **It means that there is nothing particularly to be concerned about.**

POINT
➡ It is often used in the form "*tokuni ~ nai*" such as "*tokuni ukabanai,*" "*tokuni hoshikunai.*"

---

❶ With a friend

A：明日(あした)、予定(よてい)ある？
B：ううん、**特(とく)にない**。どうしたの？

A: Do you have any plans for tomorrow?
B: No, not really. What's your plan?

❷ When you visit someone's house

A：苦手(にがて)なものある？
B：いえ、**特(とく)にありません**。何(なん)でも食(た)べられます。

A: Is there anything you can't eat?
B: No, nothing in particular. I can eat anything.

❸ A shop clerk and a customer

A：ほかに何(なに)かご要望(ようぼう)はございますか。
B：いえ、**特(とく)にありません**。

A: Do you have any other requests?
B: No, not really.

❹ Before going to a convenience store

A：コンビニに行(い)ってくるけど、何(なに)か欲(ほ)しいものある？
B：いや、**特(とく)には**。

A: I am going to the convenience store. Do you want anything?
B: Not really.

❺ In a class

A：何(なに)か質問(しつもん)はありますか。
B：いえ、**特(とく)には**…。

A: Do you have any questions?
B: No, not really.

135 特に問題ない *Tokuni mondai nai*

There's no particular problem; it will do.

✿ Means that there is no significant problem that needs to be addressed.

POINT

➡ This phrase may imply that "it's not particularly wonderful but it will do," so it should be avoided in some situations (such as when evaluating someone's cooking or new hairstyle).

❶ About a new work

A：新しい仕事、うまくいってる？
B：うん、**特に問題ない**よ。

A: Is the new job going well?
B: It's okay.

❷ Before getting an injection

A：体調はどうですか。
B：**特に問題ない**です。

A: How is your health?
B: I'm basically healthy.

❸ About a plan

A：計画は順調ですか。
B：ええ。**特に問題はありません**。

A: Is the plan proceeding smoothly?
B: Yes. We haven't run into any major problems.

❹ About a new PC

A：新しいパソコン、調子はどうですか。
B：今のところ、**特に問題ありません**。

A: How is your new PC working out?
B: It's okay so far.

❺ About a sample

A：サンプル、見てもらえましたか。
B：ええ、見ましたよ。**特に問題はありませんでした**。

A: Did you look at the sample?
B: Yes, I did. It looked okay.

136 どっちもどっちだ

Docchi mo docchi da

Neither is better than the other

❖ Indicates that neither is much better than the other, while implying that both are not especially good.

POINT

▶▶ Used in situations where there does not seem to be much point in asking which is better or worse.

❶ In a store

A：どっちが似合う？
B：う〜ん。**どっちもどっちだ**な。ちょっと派手すぎる。

A: Which one looks better?
B: Hmm. They're both about the same, a little too flashy.

❷ About friends

A：またトニーとケンカしたよ。彼はすぐ怒るから。
B：マイケルもでしょ。**どっちもどっちだ**よ。

A: I quarreled with Tony again. He has a short temper.
B: So do you, Michael. Your temper is no better than his.

Variations

❸ About cost

A：東京まで新幹線と飛行機だとどっちが安いかな？
B：ん〜、**どっちもどっち**じゃない？

A: Is it cheaper to get to Tokyo by bullet train or airplane?
B: Isn't it about the same?

❹ At a workplace

A：マネージャーには言わないほうがよかった？
B：いや、**どっちもどっちだ**ね。大して変わらない。

A: Would it have been better not to tell the manager?
B: No, it's six of one, half dozen of the other. It wouldn't have made much difference.

151

137 取り返しがつかない

Torikaeshi ga tsukanai

There's no taking that back

✿ To be in an irreversible situation.

POINT
➡ (1) Used when feeling impatient or unsure because you will feel very regretful unless you act immediately.
(2) Used when in despair over a large failure.

❶ About someone who uploaded their personal information to the internet

A：山田さん、なんでアップしちゃったんだろう。
B：もう**取り返しがつかない**よ。

A: Why do you think Yamada-san uploaded her information?
B: There's no taking that back.

❷ At the workplace

A：どうしよう。**取り返しがつかない**ミスをしたよ。
B：まだなんとかなるよ。諦めないで。

A: What should I do? I made a mistake that can't be taken back.
B: It'll work out somehow. Don't give up yet.

❸ An emergency response

A：すぐに救急車を呼んで正解だったね。
B：うん。**取り返しのつかない**ことにならなくて、本当によかった。

A: It was right to call an ambulance right away.
B: Yes. It's a good thing that something that could never be taken back didn't happen.

❹ Warning

A：そのうち、やろうと思ってるけど。
B：何言ってるの!? 今やらないと**取り返しがつかなく**なるよ。

A: I'm thinking of doing it sooner or later.
B: What're you saying?! If you don't do it now, there's no taking it back.

❺ A large failure

A：彼女に**取り返しのつかない**ことをしちゃった。
B：えっ、一体何したの？

A: I did something I can't take back to my girlfriend.
B: What? What did you do?

138 なかなか *Nakanaka*

Not bad / I'm impressed

❋ It is used to express when the evaluation is pretty good, or at a pretty high level.

POINT
➡ It is used to express when one is surprised in a good way like "over an expectation or assumption."

---

❶ New software game

A：あのゲームどうだった？
B：うん、**なかなか**だった。今度貸そうか。

A: How was that game?
B: Ya, not bad. Shall I lend it to you next time?

❷ About the flavor

A：このケーキどう？ **なかなか**じゃない？
B：うん、すごくおいしい！

A: How is this cake? Pretty good, huh?
B: Wow! It's absolutely amazing.

❸ At the workplace

A：今回のは**なかなか**いいね。
B：ありがとうございます！

A: You did a great job this time!
B: Thank you very much.

❹ About a newcomer

A：中田さん、**なかなか**やりますね。
B：ええ。見た目の印象はずいぶん大人しいんですけどね。

A: I'm impressed by Nakada-san.
B: Yes, he looks very quiet and timid, though.

139 泣きたくなる *Nakitakunaru*

It makes me want to cry

🌸 A phrase used when something is so painful it makes one want to cry.

POINT

➡ While it is sometimes used when one is actually about to cry, it is also used to simply emphasize how difficult or painful something is.

➡ It can also be used to express something that is so emotionally touching that one is moved to tears.

---

❶ A cancelation

A：せっかくここまでやったのに中止なんて、泣きたくなるよ。

B：ほんとだよね。

A: We went this far but it still got canceled. It makes me want to cry.

B: Yes, you're right.

❷ After a test

A：また試験失敗したよ。もう、泣きたくなる。

B：まだ結果も出てないし、考えるのやめようよ。

A: I messed up on yet another test. It makes me want to cry.

B: We haven't even gotten our results yet. You should stop thinking about it.

❸ At the workplace

A：あ～あ、今日も遅くなりそうだね。

B：ですね。ちょっと泣きたくなりますよね。

A: Oh, it looks like we'll be here until late today as well.

B: It does. It kind of makes you want to cry, doesn't it?

❹ A baby that won't stop crying

A：赤ちゃんが全然泣き止まないの。こっちまで泣きたくなる。

B：代わるから、ちょっと休んだら？

A: My baby won't ever stop crying. It's even making me feel like I want to cry myself.

B: I'll take over for you, so why don't you take a little break?

❺ About a famous tourist spot

A：すごく楽しみにしてたのに、工事中で見(ら)れなかったなかったよ。もう、泣きたくなった。

B：そうなんだ。残念だったね。

A: I was looking forward to it so much, but we couldn't see it because of construction. Oh, it made me want to cry.

B: Is that so. That's too bad.

140 情けない (なさ) *Nasakenai*

Pitiful

❂ Used to express feelings of sadness when a result or a situation is so awful that one cannot even feel sympathy.

POINT
- Used both to describe yourself and others.
- Also used to encourage someone to "Get their act together."

---

❶ Reflection / Regret

A：こんなミスをするなんて…。ほんと、**情けない**。

B：誰だってミスはするよ。

A: I can't believe I'd make a mistake like this... It's truly pitiful.
B: We all make mistakes sometimes.

❷ What's expected of university students

A：大学生なのに、こんな字も書けないの？ **情けない**なあ。

B：これぐらいは書けないとね。

A: What kind of university student can't even write this character? That's pitiful.
B: He ought to be able to write this at the very least.

❸ What's expected of adults

A：あの人、マナーがなさすぎる。

B：ほんと、ほんと。いい年をして**情けない**ね。

A: That person has no manners whatsoever.
B: You're absolutely right. And at that age, too. How pitiful.

❹ Don't cry

A：**情けない**なあ。ちょっと失敗したくらいで泣かないで。

B：うん…。

A: How pitiful. Don't cry just over a little mistake.
B: Okay...

❺ Reflection / Regret

A：親に迷惑ばかりかけて、自分でも**情けない**です。

B：ほんとだよ。しっかりしてよ。

A: I cause nothing but trouble for my parents. I feel pitiful myself.
B: You're absolutely right. Get your act together.

141 納得いかない *Nattoku ikanai*

Hard to accept; doesn't seem righ

❀ Indicates dissatisfaction with someone's idea, a result of something, or an event.

POINT
▶ It can mean not wanting to follow the other person's wishes.

---

❶ Additional paying

A：結局、あと300円払わなきゃいけないってこと？
B：なんか**納得いかない**ね。

A: So in the end, you have to pay another 300 yen?
B: Somehow it seems unreasonable.

❷ At a dance studio

A：今回の評価どうだった？　私はB。
B：私も。でも、リサさんがAでしょ。ちょっと**納得いかない**。

A: What grade did you get? I got a B.
B: Me too. But Lisa got an A. It doesn't quite seem right.

❸ Responsibility

A：結局、私とあなたのミスだって、部長に言われた。
B：えー、そんなの**納得いかない**よ。

A: Ultimately, the manager was told that you and I are to blame.
B: I can't accept that.

❹ At a restaurant

A：この程度の料理でこの値段は**納得いかない**ね。
B：ちょっとね…。

A: The price is unreasonably high for food of this caliber.
B: Kind of, yeah.

❺ Again from the first

A：うーん…。どうも**納得いかない**なあ。もう一回やり直しだ。
B：えっ、これ捨てちゃうの？　もったいない。

A: Hmm. It's really not acceptable. Do it over again.
B: And throw this one out? What a waste.

142 何？ *Nani?*
なに

What is it?

1: An expression used to ask what's being talked in reply to someone starting a conversation.
2: Used to express feelings of doubt, displeasure, or anger at someone's actions or a witnessed occurrence.

POINT
➡ Said forcefully when dissatisfied or irritated.

❶ Speaking to someone
A：ねえ、ちょっといい？
B：何？

A: Hey, do you have a second?
B: What is it?

❷ A task
A：〈生徒に〉ビルさん、ちょっと来てください。
B：はい、何ですか。

A: (To a student) Bill-san, can you come with me for a minute?
B: Yes, what is it?

❸ Telling someone to stop
A：ちょっと待って。
B：何!? 急いでるんだけど。

A: Hold on a second.
B: What is it!? I'm in a hurry.

❹ Looking dissatisfied
A：何？ 何か言いたそうだね。
B：ううん、別に。

A: What is it? It looks like you want to say something.
B: No, not really.

❺ Someone's attitude
A：さっきの態度は何!? すごい不愉快！
B：ごめん。悪かったよ。

A: What's with your attitude!? It's really unpleasant!
B: Sorry, that was my fault.

157

143 何が言いたいの？ *Nani ga iitai no?*

What are you trying to say?

❖ Used to request clarification of the other person's conclusion or main ideas, in a somewhat critical tone.

POINT
➡ Often used along with "after all" or "to sum up."

---

① Comparison

A：まり子さんの前の髪型、好きだったな。
B：えっ、**何が言いたいの？** 今の髪型がよくないってこと？

A: I liked the hairstyle you had before, Mariko.
B: What do you mean? Are you saying my current hairstyle is bad?

② Not want to go

A：結局、**何が言いたいの？**
B：うん…。だから、あんまり行きたくないんだよ。

A: So what are you really saying?
B: Well… you see, I don't really want to go.

③ Hard to explain

A：いや、そういうことじゃなくて…。うーん…。
B：何？ **何が言いたいの？**

A: No, that's not what I mean… uh…
B: What? What are you trying to say?

Variations -

④ Theme

A：この映画、結局**何が言いたいんだろう**。
B：うーん。いまいち、よくわからなかったね。

A: I wonder what this movie is actually trying to say.
B: I didn't really understand it very well.

144 何もなければいいけど
なに

Nani mo nakereba ii kedo

I hope nothing happens

❋ Expresses the hope that things will go well and no problems will arise in situations of anxiety or concern.

POINT
- It may be used regarding a currently existing situation or a possible future situation.
- Here, "*nani* (anything)" refers to some undesirable outcome.

❶ A Typhoon is coming

A：雨と風がだんだん強くなってきたね。
B：今回の台風はすごく大きいんでしょ？
　　何もなければいいけど。

A: The rain and wind have gotten stronger and stronger.
B: The next typhoon is supposed to be really big, isn't it. I hope it's OK.

❷ Worry about their safety

A：みんな無事に着いたのかなあ。
B：全然連絡来ないね。何もなければいいけど。

A: I wonder if they all have arrived safely.
B: There hasn't been any word at all. I hope nothing has happened.

❸ Appointment

A：じゃ、明日、７時に駅ね。ちゃんと来(ら)れそう？
B：たぶん。明日、何もなければいいけど。

A: So let's meet at the station tomorrow at 7. Will you be able to make it?
B: Probably. I hope nothing comes up tomorrow.

❹ A worry

A：検査、明日だよね？ 何もなければいいんだけど。
B：大丈夫だよ。元気すぎるぐらいだから。

A: You're having that test done tomorrow, right? I hope it's nothing.
B: It'll be fine. I'm almost too healthy.

159

145 何やってるの？ *Nani yatteru no?*

What are you doing? ; What are you up to?

✿ It is an expression used when inquiring what the other person is doing.

POINT
- It is even used when inquiring about a habitual behavior.
- If you raise the tone, it would show that you are accusing the action of the other person.

❶ At home

A：楽しそうだね。何やってるの？
B：ルーシーの誕生日会の準備だよ。

A: You seem to be having a lot of fun. What's going on?
B: We're preparing a birthday party for Lucy.

❷ How to spend a holiday

A：休みの日は何やってるの？
B：スポーツジムに行くことが多いです。

A: What do you do on holidays?
B: I go to the sport gym a lot.

❸ At home

A：何をやってるの？
B：今日は僕が料理を作ろうと思って…。

A: What are you doing?
B: Well, I was thinking of cooking today.

❹ Meeting a friend at the park

A：こんなところで何やってるんですか。
B：ああ。花の写真を撮ってるんですよ。

A: Hi, what are you doing here?
B: Oh, I'm taking pictures of flowers.

146 何よ / 何だよ　*Nani yo / Nan da yo*

Seriously?; What is it?

✿ Used to express feelings of doubt, displeasure, or anger at someone's actions or a witnessed occurrence.

POINT
➡ "*Nani yo*" is primarily used by women, while "*Nan da yo*" is primarily used by men.

---

❶ Something I want to show you

A：ちょっと見せたい物があるんだけど。
B：えー、何よ。

A: Hey, there's something I want to show you.
B: Huh? What is it?

❷ Made it in time for the train, but...

A：遅れないでよ。これに乗れないと大変なことになったんだから！
B：何よ！　いつも遅れて来るくせに！

A: You shouldn't be late. It would have been terrible if we couldn't catch this train!
B: Seriously? You're always late!

❸ A new store

A：何だよ。商品、たったこれだけ？
B：ちょっとがっかりだね。

A: Seriously? This is all they have here?
B: It's a little disappointing, isn't it?

❹ Hard rain

A：何よ、この雨！　これじゃ、外歩けないよ。
B：ほんとだね。すごいどしゃ降り。

A: What's with this rain!? We can't go outside with it like this.
B: You're right. It's pouring.

❺ A referee's call

A：何だよ、あの審判！　全然フェアじゃないじゃん。
B：うん。おかしいよ。

A: What was with that call!? There's no way it was fair.
B: Yeah. That's not right.

❻ Can't put this here

A：ここにこんな物置かないでよ！
B：何だよ、さっきから文句ばっかり言って！

A: Don't put something like that here!
B: What's your problem? You've been complaining nonstop!

161

147 何を考えているんですか
Nani o kangaeteiru n desu ka

What are you thinking?

🌸 An expression used when one cannot sympathize with and understand how another person is thinking.

POINT
- Used to express criticism, shock, anger, and so on regarding someone's remarks.
- Informal ways to say this include "*Nani kangaete ru/n no!*" or "*Nani kangaete (ru) n da!*".

❶ In front of a child

A：ちょっと！ 子供のそばでタバコを吸うなんて、一体何を考えているんですか！
B：あなたには関係ないでしょ。

A: Hey! What in the world are you thinking, smoking a cigarette next to a child like that!
B: What does it have to do with you?

Variations -

❷ Hurt, but...

A：けががまだ治ってないのに試合に出るなんて、何考えてんの！
B：今日は大事な試合なんだよ。

A: What are you thinking, playing in the game even though your injury hasn't healed yet!?
B: Today is an important match.

❸ The day before a test

A：今からカラオケ行かない？
B：明日、試験なのに!? 何考えてんの！

A: Want to go to karaoke now?
B: Even though tomorrow's the test!? What're you thinking!?

❹ Illegal dumping

A：こんなところにゴミを置いて！ 一体何を考えてるんだ！
B：非常識だよね。

A: Someone put trash here? What are they thinking!?
B: They don't have any common sense.

❺ A troubling person

A：みんな心配してるのに。何考えてんのかなあ、まったく！
B：困った人だね。

A: Look at how much everyone is worried about her Really, what is she thinking?
B: What a troubling person.

148 悩む *Nayamu*

I can't choose. I can't decide.

❀ By thinking over different options or possibilities of how best to handle things, the decision-making is difficult.

POINT
▶▶ This is casually used in daily situations.

---

❶ What to choose at a restaurant

A：おすしとてんぷら、どっちにする？
B：うーん、悩むなあ。

A: Sushi or tempura, which do you prefer?
B: Umm, I can't decide.

❷ What to wear today

A：この季節は何を着ていくか、いつも悩む。
B：私もです。

A: I can't decide what to wear, especially in this season.
B: Me neither.

❸ Choosing which school to go

A：どの学校にするか、もう決めた？
B：まだ。結構悩む。

A: Have you decided which school to go to?
B: Not yet. It's difficult for me to decide.

❹ At a store

A：まだ悩んでるの？　もう両方買ったら？
B：そんなわけにはいかないよ。ちょっと待って。

A: You haven't decided which one to choose. How about buying them both?
B: I can't do that. Give me a bit more time.

❺ Design proposals

A：これ、悩みますね。どっちもいいですもんね。
B：そうなんですよ。

A: It's difficult to choose. Both of these are good.
B: That's true.

149 なんかあったの?

Nanka attano?

Did something happen?

❋ An expression used to ask about a situation when it seems different from how it usually is.

POINT

➡ While "*Nani ga attano?*" is used to ask for details when something is clearly amiss, "*Nanika atta no?*" is used to ask whether something unusual has happened.

❶ Going home early

A：お帰り。あれ？今日は早いね。**なんかあったの？**

B：ううん。いつもより仕事が早く終わっただけ。

A: Welcome back. Hm? You're early today. Did something happen?
B: No, I just finished work earlier than usual, that's all.

❷ Looking happy

A：にやにやして、**なんかあったの？**

B：うん、ちょっといいことがね。また今度話すよ。

A: Did something happen? You're grinning.
B: Yeah, something nice. I'll tell you next time.

❸ A sudden call

A：珍しいね、電話してくるなんて。**なんかあったの？**

B：うん…。ちょっと相談したいことがあって。

A: It's not like you to call out of the blue. Did something happen?
B: Well... There's something I wanted to ask you about.

❹ When the atmosphere feels different

A：ねえ、**なんかあったの？**

B：さっき森さんと原さんが言い合いになって…。

A: Hey, did something happen?
B: Mori-san and Hara-san just got in an argument...

Variations

❺ Waiting for someone

A：スミスさん、遅いね。

B：うん…。**なんかあったのかなあ。**

A: Smith-san is late.
B: Yeah... I wonder if something happened to him.

150 なんだかなあ *Nandaka naa*

I don't get it

✿ **It shows a vague sense of discontent.**

POINT

▸ A shortened expression of "*nandaka (nandaka (nantonaku) + [shinpai da / iya da / nattoku dekinai])*."

---

❶ Am I the only one who is guilty?

A：結局、ぼく一人が悪いってこと？ **なんだかなあ**。

B：そんなことないよ。

A: You mean I am the only guilty one? I don't get it.
B: I don't mean that.

❷ A selfish president

A：社長がやっぱりやめるって。ほんと、気分次第。

B：また？ **なんだかなあ**。

A: The president is calling it off after all. He's so fickle, isn't he?
B: Behaving like that again? I don't get it.

❸ Feeling unappreciated

A：こんなに働いてるのに旅行にも行けない。**なんだかなあ**。

B：そのうち、よくなるよ。

A: We have been working this hard, and can't even go on vacation. I don't get it.
B: Things will get better soon.

❹ Being treated unfairly

A：みんな頑張ってるのに、評価されるのはいつも彼女ばっかり。

B：**なんだかね**。

A: All of us are doing our best, but she is the only one who receives praise.
B: I don't get it.

165

151 何て言ったらいいか

Nante ittara ii ka

What should I say; I don't know what to say; How do I put it

❖ Used when you want to express your emotions but don't know how to.

POINT

➡ Often used in situations where it is hard to find the correct words, such as when you are trying to communicate feeling grateful or moved, or when you are trying to comfort someone feeling pain or sadness.

❶ The taste of a drink

A：そのお酒はどんな味なの？
B：何て言ったらいいか…。リンゴのような甘みがあったよ。

A: What does that drink taste like?
B: How do I put it... It tasted sweet, like apples.

❷ A frightening moment

A：怖かったでしょ？　その時。
B：何て言ったらいいか…。「ああ、もうこれで死ぬのか…」と思いました。

A: Weren't you scared then/
B: How do I put it... I thought that "Oh, so this is how I'm going to die"...

❸ At a farewell party

A：じゃ、元気で。頑張ってね。
B：先生には本当に…。何て言ったらいいか…ありがとうございました。

A: Then be well. Do your best.
B: Oh, sensei, you're truly... I don't know what to say... Thank you.

❹ At a funeral

A：この度は本当に…何と言ったらいいか…。
B：わざわざお越しいただき、ありがとうございます。

A: I'm really... I don't know what to say...
B: Thank you very much for coming all the way here.

Variations

❺ To a friend who can't enter a competition because of an injury

A：何て言ったらいいかわからないけど、頑張って早くよくなってね。
B：うん。ありがとう。

A: I don't know what to say, but do your best to get well soon.
B: Yeah. Thank you.

152 何てことだ *Nante koto da*

I can't believe it

❁ Used to express feelings of shock or disappointment at an unfortunate result or happening.

POINT
- ▶▶ "*Nante kotta*" is an informal way of saying this.
- ▶▶ "*Nantoiu koto da*" is a slightly formal way of saying this.

❶ At the museum

A: 何てことだよ。せっかくここまで来たのに工事中だなんて。
B: ついてないね。

A: I can't believe it. We came all the way here but it's under construction?
B: What bad luck.

❷ Sold out

A: 何てことだよ。一個も残ってないなんて。
B: 今、一番売れる時期だからね。しょうがないよ。

A: I can't believe it. There's not a single one left?
B: This is the time of year when they're the most popular. There's nothing you can do about it.

Variations

❸ Before going out

A: 何てこった。ズボンに穴が空いてるよ。これじゃ、はいていけない。
B: あ、ほんとだ。それはかっこ悪いね。

A: I can't believe it. There's a hole in my pants. I can't wear these.
B: Oh, you're right. Yes, that wouldn't look cool.

❹ After a trip

A: えー、何てこと！ 花が全部枯れてる！
B: ああ…残念だね。

A: Oh, I can't believe it! All of my flowers have wilted!
B: Oh... That's too bad.

153 何でもない Nandemonai

It's nothing

🌸 Used to express feelings that there's nothing worth mentioning or nothing of note that has happened.

POINT
- Often used in response to someone who asks "Are you okay?" because they notice that something is unusual.
- Often used when there is something that one actually wants others to ask about but is going out of their way not to discuss it.

❶ B is staring at A

A：ん？　何？
B：あ、ううん、何でもない。

A: Huh? What is it?
B: Oh, no. It's nothing.

❷ B is crying

A：大丈夫？　どうしたの？
B：大丈夫。何でもない。

A: Are you okay? What happened?
B: I'm fine. It's nothing.

❸ How someone else is acting

A：何か言いたいことがあるんじゃないの？
B：何でもないって。

A: There's something you want to say, isn't there?
B: It's nothing, really.

❹ Doesn't it actually hurt?

A：本人は「これくらい何でもない」って。
B：何でもないってことはないでしょ。相当痛いと思うよ。

A: He was saying that "this is nothing".
B: There's no way that was nothing. I think it must be quite painful.

❺ How a computer is working

A：パソコン、壊れちゃったの？
B：いや、別に何でもなかった。すぐ元に戻ったよ。

A: Did your computer break?
B: No, it's nothing, really. It went back to normal in no time.

154 何とも言えない *Nantomo ienai*

There's nothing I can say; I don't know what to say

❁ A phrase used when one is in the position of being unable to say anything with certainty, or has feelings to that extent.

POINT
➡ Often used when one wishes to neither give a positive or negative answer.

❶ Tomorrow's weather

A：この様子じゃ、明日も雨かなあ。
B：うーん、**何とも言えない**なあ。

A: At this rate, it looks like it'll rain tomorrow too.
B: Hmm, I don't know what to say.

❷ At the hospital

A：先生、私はいつごろ退院できるでしょうか。
B：検査結果を見ないと、**何とも言えません**ね。

A: Sensei, when will I be able to leave the hospital.
B: There's nothing I can say until I look at the test results.

❸ On the phone

A：今日は何時ごろに帰れそう？
B：うーん…。夕方から会議でさあ。**何とも言えない**な。

A: When do you think you'll be able to return home today?
B: Hmm... Well, I have a meeting from the evening. I don't know what to say.

❹ Who threw it?

A：きっと彼がここにごみを捨てたんだよ。そう思わない？
B：いやあ、直接見たわけじゃないから、**何とも言えない**よ。

A: He probably threw his trash out here. Don't you think?
B: Well, it's not like I saw it with my own eyes. There's nothing I can say.

❺ Which is faster?

A：地下鉄よりタクシーのほうが早いかなあ。
B：**何とも言えない**なあ。道、込んでるからね。

A: I wonder if it'd be faster to take a taxi than to take the subway.
B: I don't know what to say. The streets are crowded.

❻ In a troubling situation

A：全部彼のせいと言うつもりはないんだけど…。困りました。
B：そうですか。私は事情を知らないので**何とも言えません**が。

A: I don't mean to blame everything on him, but... I don't know what to do.
B: I see. Of course, I don't know anything about the circumstances, so there's nothing I can say.

169

155 ばかばかしい *Bakabakashii*

Absurd; pointless

✿ Used to express one's feelings that something is completely meaningless, useless, or worthless.

POINT
➡ Sometimes used as a careless comment when something would normally have value but seems meaningless due to the situation.
➡ "*Bakarashii*" is also often used with the same meaning.

① Using money

A：ギャンブルにお金を使うなんて**ばかばかしい**よ。
B：自分のお金なんだから、別にいいじゃない。

A: It's pointless to use your money gambling.
B: It's my money, I don't see the problem.

② Using money

A：こんなものに税金を使うなんて、ほんと、**ばかばかしい**と思う。
B：ほんとだよね。

A: Using taxes on this seems completely absurd.
B: You're right.

③ At work

A：また席替えするんだって。
B：また？ 時間の無駄だよ。**ばかばかしい**。

A: I hear they're shuffling desks around again.
B: Again? What a waste of time. It's pointless.

④ Displeasure

A：自分が損するばかりで、こんな**ばかばかしい**ことはないよ。
B：そうだね。

A: There's nothing positive that could come out of this for you. Why would you do something this absurd?
B: You're right.

⑤ At work

A：一生懸命やってるのに、客には文句ばかり言われて、**ばかばかしく**なってきた。
B：そんなことないよ。感謝してくれるお客さんもいるじゃない。

A: I work so hard yet all I ever get is complaints from customers. This seems pointless.
B: That's not true. Some customers thank you, don't they?

156 ばかみたい *Baka mitai*

That seems ridiculous

✿ Used to express that you feel someone's actions or the state of a situation is foolish.

POINT

➡ Not only used about others, but about one's self as well. In such cases, it is frequently used in situations that feel irrational because only you are at a disadvantage.

❶ About a friend

A：彼、一人で大騒ぎして、**ばかみたい**。
B：ほんとだね。

A: He's getting all worked up on his own, it seems ridiculous.
B: You're absolutely right.

❷ My troubles

A：彼の言葉に私ばかり悩んでて、**ばかみたい**です。
B：もう忘れたほうがいいよ。

A: I'm worried all by myself about what he said, it seems ridiculous.
B: You should just forget it.

❸ A failed purchase

A：こんなのに高いお金払ったの？**ばかみたい**。
B：でも、もう買っちゃったからなあ。

A: You spent a lot of money on something like this? It seems ridiculous.
B: But I already bought it, so...

Variations --

❹ Feelings of not being good enough

A：頑張れば頑張るほど自分が損するなんて、**ばかみたいな**話ですね。
B：ええ。

A: The more I try, the worse off I am. It's ridiculous, isn't it?
B: Yes.

❺ Something being asked

A：**ばかみたいな**質問かもしれないけど、聞いていい？
B：何？

A: This may seem like a ridiculous question, but may I ask you something?
B: What is it?

157 恥ずかしい *Hazukashii*

I'm ashamed; It's embarrassing

❀ It is used to express your feeling of being ashamed or embarrassed about your own faults or misbehavior.

POINT

➡ It is used as an accusation if you say, "*Hazukashikunai no?* (Aren't you ashamed of yourself?)".

---

❶ Adult's commonsense

A：この漢字、なんて読むの？
B：えっ？ それが読めないのは、ちょっと恥ずかしいよ。

A: How do you read this Kanji-character?
B: Unbelievable! You should be ashamed of yourself if you can't read that.

❷ Can't cook

A：得意料理とか、あるんですか。
B：お恥ずかしい話ですが、料理は全然だめなんです。

A: Do you have any special dish you cook best?
B: I'm embarrassed to admit it, but I can't cook at all.

❸ After causing trouble to someone

A：あんなことして、恥ずかしくないの？
B：悪かったと思ってるよ。

A: Aren't you ashamed of having done such a thing?
B: Yeah, I'm ashamed of myself.

❹ Illegal parking

A：自転車、持っていかれたの？
B：お恥ずかしい話です。停めたらいけない場所だったんです。

A: Was your bicycle towed away?
B: Shame on me. I was not supposed to park there.

158 はっきりして *Hakkiri shite*

Be more clear

1: Used to indicate that someone's vague attitude is a problem.
2: Used to communicate feelings of irritation due to a situation being stagnant.

POINT
➡ Often used together with an interrogative, such as "A *ka* B *ka* + *hakkiri shite*" "~ *ka doo ka* + *hakkiri shite hoshii*."

❶ Before going out

A：何やってるの!?　行くのか、行かないのか、**はっきりして**。
B：行くよ。ちょっと待って。

A: What're you doing?! Be more clear whether you're going or not.
B: I'm going. Just wait a second.

Variations

❷ Present or absent

A：原さんって、出席か欠席か、まだ決めてないんだ。
B：そうなんですよ。でも、**はっきりして**くれないと困ります。

A: So Hara-san hasn't decided whether he'll be present or not?
B: That's right. But it'll be a problem if he's not clear about it.

❸ Feelings for a girlfriend

A：彼女のことが好きなのか、どうなのか、**はっきりしろ**よ。
B：ああ、好きだよ。

A: You need to be clear on whether or not you love her.
B: Yeah, I love her.

❹ Details of a job

A：結局、私たちは何をすればいいの？
B：よくわかんない。**はっきりしてほしい**よね。

A: So what do we even need to do?
B: I'm not sure. I wish they'd be clear.

159 初耳です *Hatsumimi desu*

The first I've heard of it

✿ Used to express that you are hearing something someone is saying for the first time.

POINT

➡ Often used when one feels a sense of surprise or unexpected shock.

---

❶ At a party

A: あれ？ 資料持ってどこ行くんですか。会議は明日に延期ですよ。
B: えっ、そうなんですか!? 初耳ですよ。

A: Huh? Where are you going with those materials? The meeting was delayed until tomorrow.
B: What, it is?! That's the first I've heard of it.

❷ A colleague's marriage

A: 森さんの結婚祝い、何にしようか。
B: えっ？ 森さん、結婚するの!? 初耳だよー。

A: What should we do for Mori-san's wedding gift?
B: What? Mori-san is getting married?! That's the first I've heard of it!

❸ At a part-time job

A: 明日の勤務シフト変わったの、聞いてる？
B: えっ、何それ？ そんなの初耳だよ。

A: Did you hear that tomorrow's work shifts changed?
B: What, seriously? That's the first I've heard of it.

❹ Hometown

A: これ、実家の青森から送ってきたリンゴです。よかったらどうぞ。
B: 田中さん、青森出身だったんですか。それは初耳です。

A: These are apples I was sent from my home in Aomori. Please have some if you'd like.
B: You were born in Aomori-Tanaka-san? I never knew that before.

❺ About moving

A: 来月引っ越すって、話したっけ？
B: いや、初耳だよ。どこに引っ越すの？

A: Did I tell you I was moving next month?
B: No, that's the first I've heard of it. Where are you moving to?

160 話が違う　*Hanashi ga chigau*

Not what I've heard

❖ Used to point out that the point or content of something is different from what one heard or thought before and to express dissatisfaction.

POINT

➡ Used to express feelings that the conditions regarding something are different and therefore one cannot accept things as-is.

❶ New workplace

A：じゃ、来週からお願いしたいんですが、月・水・金と土曜日でいいですか。
B：えっ、土曜日もですか!? ちょっと**話が違う**んですけど。

A: So I'd like to ask you to start beginning next week, but how does Monday, Wednesday, Friday, and Saturday sound?
B: What? Saturday, too?! I never heard about that.

❷ Present

A：彼女、プレゼント喜んでた？
B：うーん…。店員は絶対大喜びするって言ってたけど、なんか**話が違った**な。

A: Did your girlfriend like the present you got her?
B: Well... The employee at the store said she would be sure to love it, but it didn't exactly go that way.

❸ Test

A：テスト範囲、20ページから80ページまでだって。
B：えっ、60ページまでじゃないの!? **話が違う**よー！

A: I heard the test covers from page 20 to page 80.
B: What? Not to page 60?! That's not what I heard!

❹ Price

A：では、代金の20万円と別途消費税を頂戴します。
B：えっ？ 税込で20万円って聞きましたよ。**話が違います**。

A: That will be 200,000 yen plus sales tax, please.
B: What? I was told 200,000 yen including tax. That's not what I heard.

❺ Responsibility for consequences

A：ミスは申し訳ないですが、一生懸命やってますので。
B：それはわかってます。でも、それとこれとは**話が違います**。

A: I apologize about the mistakes, but I'm doing my best.
B: I understand that. But that's not what I'm talking about right now.

❻ Promising to meet

A：ごめん、やっぱり金曜日行けなくなった。
B：えー、**話が違う**じゃない！ 金曜日なら大丈夫って言うから変えたのに。

A: Sorry, I can't go on Friday after all.
B: What, that's not what you said earlier! I changed it to Friday because you said it would be fine.

175

161 ひどくない? *Hidokunai?*

Isn't it awful?; Can you believe it?

🌸 Used to express a desire for sympathy when speaking to someone about an excessively bad situation or when someone's words and actions are cold and cruel.

POINT

➡ Can be used to speak of both situations and people, but the meaning changes in these situations as described above.

❶ Animal abuse

A：この写真見て。**ひどくない？**
B：何これ!?　ひどすぎる！

A: Look at this picture. Isn't it awful?
B: What is this!? It's completely awful!

❷ At a restaurant

A：こんな料理で 2000 円なんて、**ひどくない？**
B：これはちょっとねえ…。

A: 2,000 yen for food like this? Can you believe that?
B: That's a little much for this...

❸ At work

A：この取扱説明書、**ひどくない？**　すごい不親切。
B：安物だからね。しょうがないよ。

A: Isn't this user's manual awful? How unhelpful.
B: It was a cheap buy, what can you do?

❹ How a match went

A：昨日の試合、見た？　ちょっと**ひどくない？**
B：うん、あれはひどいね。

A: Did you watch yesterday's match? Wasn't it kind of awful?
B: Yeah, it was terrible.

❺ About a boss

A：人のことをばかとか使えないとか、**ひどくないですか。**
B：そうだね。ちょっとひどいね。

A: Can you believe that he calls people "stupid" and "useless"?
B: You're right. It's not kind of him to do that.

162 他人事じゃない *Hitogoto ja nai*

This isn't someone else's problem

❋ Used to express feelings that "I'm not unrelated to that problem" or "The same kind of problem may happen to us."

POINT

▶▶ Includes feelings of the speaker (or the person being spoken to) needing to be careful.

---

❶ A problem learned about through the news

A：今はいいけど、**他人事じゃない**よね。
B：そうだね。いつ自分たちがそうなるか、わからないもんね。

A: We're okay for now, but this isn't someone else's problem.
B: That's right. You never know when it'll happen to us.

❷ A problem learned about through the news

A：これは**他人事じゃない**と思う。
B：うん。私たちも似たような立場だからね。

A: I don't think this is someone else's problem.
B: Yeah. We're in a similar situation, after all.

❸ Seeing news of an accident

A：怖いね。
B：ほんと。**他人事じゃない**よ。

A: That's scary.
B: It really is. And it's not just someone else's problem.

❹ Not understanding the situation

A：彼は自分は関係ないと思ってるのかなあ。
B：さあ…。**他人事じゃない**のにね。

A: I wonder if he thinks he's unrelated to this.
B: Who knows... But it's not someone else's problem for him.

163 一言多い (ひとことおお) *Hitokoto ooi*

(To) say too much

🌸 **Used to express feelings of displeasure when someone says something unnecessary.**

POINT
➡ Often used when something inappropriate is said that causes displeasure to or aggravates a problem with someone.

---

❶ A troubling person

A：彼はいつも**一言多い**よね。
B：そう。なんでああなんだろう。

A: He always says too much.
B: You're right. I wonder why he's like that.

❷ With a friend

A：そんなこと、今言わなくてもいいじゃない。**一言多い**んだよ。
B：そうかなあ。

A: You don't need to say something like that right now. You're saying too much.
B: I wonder.

Related phrases

❸「一言余計だ」

A：さっきのは**一言余計だった**かもしれない。
B：そうだよ。彼、ちょっとむっとしてたよ。

A: I may have said too much just now.
B: You're right. He was a little angry.

❹「一言余計だ」

A：その服、かわいいね。ちょっとサイズが小さいかもしれないけど。
B：**一言余計だ**よ。

A: Those clothes are cute. They might be a little too small for you, though.
B: You're saying too much.

164 凹む *Hekomu*

Feel depressed, depressing

✿ **To get depressed or feel down.**

POINT
➡ A more casual impression than "*ochikomu*."
➡ Originally, it meant that "boxes or metal boards have a pitted surface."

---

❶ At the office

A: データ、全部消えちゃったよ。
B: えー、全部!? それは凹むね。

A: All the data is gone.
B: Wow, all of it? That's depressing.

❷ A senior staff member gets mad at one of your colleagues

A: 彼、だいぶ凹んでるみたい。
B: あんなふうに言われたら、誰だって凹みますよ。

A: He looked very depressed.
B: Anybody would be depressed if they were talked to like that.

❸ With a friend

A: 森さんらしくないね。元気出して！
B: ぼくだって凹むことぐらいありますよ。

A: You don't look like your usual self, Mr. Mori. Cheer up!
B: Even I get depressed sometimes.

❹ Being an ineffective moderator

A: 名前を間違えて言っちゃったんです。
B: そうか。それで凹んでるんだ。

A: I called the wrong name.
B: I see. That's why you look depressed.

179

165 別に怒ってない *Betsuni okottenai*

It's not like I'm mad

✿ Used to convey that one is not mad. The phrase also includes feelings of being upset that someone would think that one was mad.

POINT

➡ Often used when one is not mad but still are upset.

❶ A trouble over trifles

A：さっきはごめん。怒ってる？
B：**別に怒ってない**よ。

A: Sorry about earlier. Are you mad?
B: It's not like I'm mad.

❷ Her feelings

A：彼女、怒ってるかなあ。どうしよう。
B：大丈夫だよ。**別に怒ってない**って。

A: I wonder if my girlfriend is mad. What should I do?
B: It's fine. I told you, it's not like she's mad.

❸ Angry?

A：本当は怒ってるんでしょ？
B：だから、**別に怒ってない**って。

A: You're actually mad at me, aren't you?
B: Like I said, it's not like I'm mad.

❹ Earnestly apologize

A：ほんとにごめん。ぼくが悪かったよ。
B：そんなに謝らないでよ。**別に怒ってない**から。

A: I'm really sorry. It was my fault.
B: Stop apologizing so much. It's not like I'm mad.

❺ Your feelings

A：マイケルが気にしてたよ。怒ってるんじゃないかって。
B：え、なんで？ **別に怒ってない**けど。

A: Michael was worried. He thought you might be mad.
B: What, why? It's not like I'm mad.

166 勉強になる *Benkyoo ni naru*

It's instructive

❋ Used to indicate positive feelings of being able to learn from or use something.

POINT
▶ Often said about something someone has said or an experience.

---

❶ A good talk

A：先生の話、面白いね。
B：うん。**勉強になる**よ。

A: Our teacher says such interesting things.
B: Yes. They're instructive.

❷ About a seminar

A：このセミナー、どうかなあ。
B：行ったことあるけど、**勉強になる**よ。

A: I wonder how this seminar is.
B: I've been before, but it'll be instructive.

❸ Something actually experienced

A：やっぱり実際に経験すると**勉強になる**ね。
B：そりゃ、そうだよ。

A: It really is instructive to actually experience something for yourself.
B: Well, of course it is.

❹ Hearing from an expert in a field

A：今日はいい話を聞かせていただき、ありがとうございました。とても**勉強になりました**。
B：そうですか。

A: Thank you very much for your talk today. It was very instructive.
B: Was it, now.

❺ After a lecture

A：こういうのに出ると、いろいろ**勉強になる**ね。
B：そうだね。

A: Going to those kinds of things is so instructive, isn't it?
B: You're right.

181

167 ぼちぼち *Bochibochi*

Getting better. Not too bad.

❃ Although not much is going on, things have slowly started to happen. This reflects the speaker's feeling that the situation is neither positive nor negative yet.

POINT
➨ This is often used in the Kansai area but it also makes sense in other regions.
➨ It is also used when the speakers want to appear humble.

❶ At office
A: 仕事はどう？ うまくいってる？
B: そうですね。**ぼちぼち**です。

A: How is work going? Is it all right?
B: Uh, getting a bit better.

❷ At college
A: 来週、レポートの締め切りだよね。準備してる？
B: **ぼちぼち**ね。

A: We have a deadline for an assignment next week. Have you started?
B: I'm beginning to do so.

❸ Schedule for construction
A: 工事は始まった？
B: まだだけど、**ぼちぼち**始まるんじゃないかな。

A: Has the construction started?
B: Not yet. But it is about to start, I think.

❹ At work
A: どうですか。売り上げのほうは？
B: そうですね。**ぼちぼち**というところですね。

A: So, how are the sales?
B: Let me see. Not too bad.

❺ At the shop your acquaintance has opened
A: 結構お客さんが来てるじゃない。
B: まあ、**ぼちぼち**かな。

A: You have lot of of customers.
B: Well, not too bad, I think.

168 ほっとく *Hottoku*

Leave ~ alone. Don't worry about ~.

✿ To leave something as it is without caring or worrying over it.

POINT
➡ ・A shortened expression of "*hootteoku*."

---

❶ About a friend

A：ヤンさん、まだ怒ってるのかな？
B：そのうち落ち着くよ。**ほっとこう**。

A: Do you think Mr. Yang is still angry?
B: He'll be all right soon. Let's leave him alone for a while.

❷ Mind your own business

A：ちょっと食べ過ぎなんじゃない？
B：別にいいでしょ？　**ほっといて**よ。

A: You're eating too much, aren't you?
B: Mind your own business. Leave me alone.

❸ Being worried

A：ちょっと一人にして。
B：こんな時に、**ほっとく**わけにはいかないよ。

A: Leave me alone.
B: This is important. I can't.

❹ Don't worry

A：マイケルがいつも私のことばかにするんです。
B：そんな人、**ほっとけば**いいよ。

A: Michael always laughs at me.
B: Don't worry about it.

169 ほっとしました Hotto shimashita

I'm relieved

✿ Indicates relief when some concern turns out to be fine or a stressful event is over.

POINT
➡ "*Hott*" indicates a sigh of relief.

---

❶ Feeling relieved

A：ご家族と連絡が取れたんですか。
B：はい。とりあえず、ほっとしました。

A: Were you able to get in touch with your family?
B: Yes. That has set my mind at ease for the time being.

❷ After a presentation

A：お疲れ様。無事に終わってよかったね。
B：うん。とりあえず、ほっとしたよ。

A: Good job. You must be glad to have that over with.
B: Yes. Anyway that's a relief.

❸ At the hospital

A：大したことなくてよかった。元気な顔が見(ら)れてほっとしたよ。
B：ご心配おかけしてすみませんでした。

A: I'm glad it wasn't anything major. It's a relief to see you looking well.
B: I'm sorry to have caused you concern.

❹ In the train

A：あー、危なかった。
B：とりあえず、ほっとしたよ。これに乗れなかったら大変なことになってたからね。

A: Wow, we almost missed it.
B: Anyway that's a relief. We'd be in trouble if we hadn't made it onto this one.

❺ Found

A：あっ、コンタクトあったよ！
B：よかった〜！　これ高いんですよ。見つかってほっとしました。

A: Oh, I found your contact lens!
B: Wonderful! This is expensive. I'm relieved that it's found.

170 ほどほどにね *Hodohodo ni ne*

Take it easy

✿ **Used to advise someone to use moderation.**

POINT

➡ "*hodohodo* (in moderation)" means just the right amount, without being excessive.

---

❶ About diet

A：最近、朝食抜いてるんだ。
B：え？ 体に良くないんじゃない？ ダイエットも**ほどほどにね**。

A: I've been going without breakfast lately.
B: Isn't that unhealthy? Even dieting should be done in moderation.

❷ At a workplace

A：じゃ、お先に。田中さんも、**ほどほどにね**。
B：私もそろそろ帰ります。お疲れ様でした。

A: I'm leaving for the day. Tanaka-san, you shouldn't overdo it either.
B: I'll knock off soon, too. You have worked hard today.

❸ Alcohol

A：ビールもう１杯飲もうかな。
B：大丈夫？ **ほどほどにして**よ。

A: I might have one more beer.
B: Are you sure? Don't drink more than you should.

❹ In a store

A：それもこれもいや。かわいくない。
B：もう！ わがままも**ほどほどにして**。

A: I don't want that one or this one. They're not cute.
B: Really! Try not to act so spoiled.

171 本気で言ってるの？
Honki de itteru no?

Are you serious?

✿ An expression to confirm how serious someone is. It often implies the speaker's doubt or disbelief about how sincere the other person is.

POINT
➡ This is often used when the other speaker adopts a serious tone.

❶ Suggestion

A: 自転車買って、日本を縦断しようよ。
B: **本気で言ってるの？** 結構大変だよ。

A: Let's buy a bicycle and travel throughout Japan.
B: Are you serious? It's not that easy.

❷ Things one wants

A: 実は会社をやめて、農業をしたいんです。
B: それ、**本気で言ってるの？** 冗談でしょ？

A: As a matter of fact, I want to quit to my job and start farming.
B: Are you serious? You must be kidding.

❸ About relationships

A: 私たち、やっぱり合わないと思う。別れたほうがいいんだよ。
B: えっ、**本気で言ってるの？**

A: We are incompatible. We'd better break up.
B: What? Are you serious?

Related phrases

❹「本気(なの)かなあ」

A: プロのボクサーを目指すなんて、彼、**本気なのかなあ**。
B: ああ、本気みたいだよ。

A: I wonder how serious he is when he says he wants to become a professional boxer.
B: Yeah, he looks serious.

172 任せた *Makaseta*

I'm leaving it to you

❖ **Used to communicate that it is alright for something to proceed as someone else sees fit.**

POINT
➡ Often used when one feels that making decisions is too much trouble or when they do not have the time or room to.

---

❶ Choosing a store

A：お店、どこにする？
B：どこでもいいよ。任せた。

A: What store should we go to?
B: Anywhere is fine. I'll leave it to you.

❷ Preparing for a party

A：じゃ、飲み物、買ってくるね。ピザの注文は任せた。
B：わかった。

A: In that case, I'll go buy drinks. I'll leave the pizza ordering to you.
B: Okay.

❸ Invitees

A：田中さんとか森さんとかも誘う？
B：うーん…。任せた。

A: Do you want to invite Tanaka-san and Mori-san as well?
B: Hmm... I'll leave that to you.

❹ Reservations

A：お店の予約もしてくれたの？
B：いや。それはスーザンに任せた。

A: Did you make store reservations too?
B: No, I left that to Susan.

173 またー *Mataa*

Oh you; again?

✿ Used to express feelings of astonishment at the words or actions of others.

POINT
➡ "*Matamataa*" can be used to say this in an even more stressed manner, and it is used to make fun of someone's modesty.

❶ Not cute

A：私は全然可愛くないからモテないですよ。
B：**またー**。誰も信じないですよ。

A: I'm not cute at all, so I'll never get a date.
B: Again? No one believes you when you say that.

❷ Compliment

A：リンダさんって、かっこいいですよね。美人で頭が良くて。
B：**またー**。調子いいんだから。

A: You're so cool, Linda-san. You're beautiful and smart.
B: Oh, you. Acting so slick.

❸ If leaving the company

A：私が辞めても、誰も困らないと思うんです。
B：**またー**。変なこと言わないで。

A: I don't think anyone at all would be troubled if I quit.
B: Again? Stop saying such weird things.

❹ Unskilled

A：僕はまだまだですよ。もっと練習しなきゃ。
B：**またー**。めちゃくちゃうまいじゃないですか。

A: I still have a long way to go. I need to practice more.
B: Oh, you. You're incredibly good.

Variations

❺ At karaoke

A：歌は下手なので、皆さんのを聞いてるだけでいいです。
B：**またまたー**。田中さんから、すごく上手だって聞いてますよ。

A: I'm a poor singer, so I'll just listen to all of you sing.
B: Oh, you. I've heard from Tanaka-san that you're a very good singer.

174 また頑張ろう *Mata ganbaroo*

Let's try again another time

1: An expression used to encourage someone to try hard next time even though the current attempt ended in failure.

2: An expression used to encourage someone to continue to try hard at work or study.

POINT
➤ Includes feelings of recognizing the hard work of the person being spoken to as well as a feeling of promising to work hard alongside them.

❶ After a match

A：今日は残念だったけど、明日から**また頑張ろう**。
B：はい。

A: It was too bad about today, but let's try hard again starting tomorrow.
B: Okay.

❷ After something sad

A：今はつらいと思うけど、**また頑張ろう**。
B：うん。

A: It might be tough now, but let's try again another time.
B: Yeah.

Variations

❸ After not passing

A：元気出して。**また頑張ればいい**よ。
B：はい。

A: Cheer up. You just have to try again.
B: Okay.

❹ Sunday, with a friend

A：明日から**また頑張りましょう**。
B：ええ。

A: Let's keep working hard starting tomorrow.
B: Yes.

❺ After receiving advice

A：いろいろアドバイスありがとうございます。**また頑張ります**。
B：ええ。頑張ってください。

A: Thank you for all the advice. I'll try again.
B: Alright. Do your best.

175 またにしよう *Mata ni shiyoo*

Let's do it another time

🌸 **An expression used to suggest doing something at the next opportunity, or to agree with such a suggestion.**

POINT
➡ A shortening of *"Mata kondo ni shiyoo."*

---

❶ A line in front of a store

A：うわ…。すごい並んでる。
B：**またにしよう**か。

A: Wow… Look at this big line.
B: Why don't we do this another time?

❷ Plans to go to the mountains

A：雨、やみそうもないね。
B：うん…。山に行くのは**またにしよう**。

A: It doesn't look like the rain is going to stop.
B: Yeah… Let's go to the mountain another time.

❸ A popular spot

A：この時期は混んでるから、**またにしよう**よ。
B：えー。またって、いつ行くのよ。今日、行っちゃおう。

A: It's crowded around this time, so let's go another time.
B: What? When's that going to be? Let's go today.

❹ A lesson

A：じゃ、この続きは**またにしましょう**。
B：はい。ありがとうございました。

A: Let's continue this another time.
B: Okay. Thank you very much.

Related phrases

❺「またにする」

A：なんか用？
B：ああ…。いいや、**またにする**。忙しそうだから。

A: Do you need something?
B: Oh… No, maybe next time. You seem busy.

176 まだまだこれからです

Madamada korekara desu

(It's) only getting started

✿ Used to express a view or feelings that "what is important is coming" or "things will become even more intense."

POINT
➡ Can be used in both positive and negative situations.

---

① Winter in Japan

A：ううう…。日本って寒いですね。
B：冬は**まだまだこれからです**よ。

A: Agh... Japan is a very cold country, isn't it?
B: The winter is only getting started.

② When eating a course meal

A：結構お腹がいっぱいになってきた。
B：えー、**まだまだこれからです**よ。

A: I'm getting pretty full.
B: What? We're only getting started.

③ Encouragement

A：一生懸命やってるつもりだけど、なかなか上達しないなあ。
B：始めたばかりじゃないですか。**まだまだこれからです**よ。

A: I feel like I'm giving this my best, but I'm not getting any better.
B: You've only just started. You're going to get better from here.

④ Passing a test

A：日本語能力試験、N3合格おめでとう！
B：ありがとうございます。でも、**まだまだこれからです**。

A: Congratulations on passing the N3 level of the Japanese Language Proficiency Test!
B: Thank you, but I'm only getting started.

⑤ A new employee

A：彼、なかなか仕事を覚えないんで、困ってるんですよ。
B：入って1か月でしょ。**まだまだこれからだ**よ。

A: He hasn't been able to learn much of the job, so he's having trouble.
B: It's only been a month since he started. He's just getting started.

177 間違ってたらごめんなさい
Machigattetara gomennasai

I'm sorry if I'm mistaken

❀ An expression used to indicate that one's understanding of something may be incorrect.

POINT
➡ Often used when making predictions or when one wishes to confirm something.

❶ Reservation time

A: 6時に予約したと思うんだけど、**間違ってたらごめんなさい**。
B: わかった。

A: I think the reservation is at 6, but I'm sorry if I'm mistaken.
B: Okay.

❷ The wrong person

A: **間違ってたらごめんなさい**。もしかして、田中さんですか。
B: いえ、違いますよ

A: I'm sorry if I'm mistaken, but are you Tanaka-san?
B: No, I'm not.

❸ The location of a key

A: 鍵、どこに置いたの？ 取ってくるよ。
B: 机の上だと思うんだけど…**間違ってたらごめんなさい**。

A: Where did you put the key? I'll go get it.
B: I think I put it on top of the desk, but...I'm sorry if I'm mistaken.

❹ A Japanese composition

A: 一生懸命書いたんですが、日本語が**間違ってたらごめんなさい**。
B: どれどれ…。大丈夫、合ってるよ。

A: I did my best to write this, but I'm sorry if the Japanese is wrong.
B: Let's take a look... Don't worry, it's fine.

❺ Materials

A: **間違ってたらごめんなさい**。この資料作ったの、森さん？
B: はい、私ですが、何か問題ありましたか。

A: I'm sorry if I'm mistaken, but did you make these materials, Mori-san?
B: Yes, I did. Is there a problem?

178 まったく *Mattaku*

For Christ's sake. Come on.

✿ This shows anger or astonishment at the behavior of another.

POINT
▶ By adding "*moo,*" it can be amplified.

---

❶ Illegal disposal

A：**まったく**！ 誰がこんな所にごみ捨てたんだよ。
B：非常識だよね。

A: For Christ's sake! Who dumped garbage here?
B: Thoughtless behavior, isn't it?

❷ An appointment

A：遅くなってごめん！
B：**まったく**、もう！ 何分待たせるつもり!?

A: Sorry to be late!
B: Come on! How long are you going to keep me waiting?!

❸ Common manners

A：**まったく**！ 挨拶ぐらい普通にやってほしいよね。
B：まあ、まあ。そう怒らないで。

A: For Christ's sake! Am I expecting too much – I just want to hear him saying hello?
B: Calm down. Don't get upset.

❹ Complaints

A：**まったく**！ なんで私がこんなことまでしなけりゃなんないの!?
B：まあ、今日は運が悪かったんだよ。

A: For Christ's sake! Why do I have to do that?!
B: Calm down. You are unlucky today.

193

179 まねできない *Mane dekinai*

No one else can do it. I can't do it.

❋ This shows an admiration for someone's skill or level of behavior, and a feeling that you cannot do likewise.

POINT
➡ The basic form is "*Watashi niwa mane dekinai.*"

❶ About a mutual acquaintance

A：リサさんって、すごい努力家だよね。
B：うん。私には**まねできない**。

A: Lisa is very hard-working.
B: Yes, I can't do what she does.

❷ A guitar performance

A：あの指の動き、すごいね。
B：うん、ちょっと**まねできない**ね。

A: That movement of fingers is amazing.
B: Agree. No one else can do it.

❸ Talent of a friend

A：マイケルの描く絵って、本当に面白い！
B：あれは誰にも**まねできない**よ。

A: Michael's paintings are really interesting!
B: No one else can do that.

❹ About the young generation

A：今の若い子のファッションって、すごいね。
B：うん。私には**まねできない**。

A: Isn't recent young people's fashion amazing?
B: Agreed. I can't do the same thing.

180 見損なった *Misokonatta*

Misjudged; lost respect

✿ Indicates having misjudged or overestimated someone.

POINT
➡ Generally used in the form of "*Misokonatta*." Indicates scorn or disappointment when one's high esteem is lost (when forming a poor impression) for some reason.
➡ Often used with regard to someone's attitude or approach rather than their abilities.

❶ Band activity

A：俺、もうバンドやめるよ。
B：プロ目指して頑張ろうって言ってたのに。見損なったよ。

A: I'm going to quit the band.
B: But you were going to practice hard and try to go pro. I'm disappointed.

❷ Unexpected remark

A：まさか、彼があんなことを言うとは思わなかった。
B：ほんと。ちょっと見損なったね。

A: I never thought he'd say something like that.
B: I know. It's kind of disappointing.

❸ The director's comment

A：負けたのを全部、選手のせいにしてるね。
B：うん。もうちょっとましな監督かと思ってたけど、見損なったな。

A: He's putting all the blame for losing on the athletes.
B: Yeah. I thought he would be a better coach than that, but I overestimated him.

❹ Cold attitude

A：人が困ってるのに、何もしてあげないなんて…。見損なったよ。
B：ちょっとがっかりだよね。

A: Not doing anything to help when people are in trouble... I would have thought better of them.
B: It's sort of disappointing, isn't it.

❺ Different from Impressions

A：彼、見た目は冷たい感じなんだけど、実は優しい人だと思う。
B：うん、ちょっと見損なってたよ。

A: He looks like a cold person, but I think that in reality he is kind.
B: Yes, I misjudged him.

181 みっともない *Mittomonai*

Not a pleasant sight

✿ This describes someone's behavior as being unpleasant to watch.

POINT
- The original form "*mitaku mo nai*" has evolved into "*mittomonai*."
- It can be also said as "*migurushii*."

❶ A drunkard

A: あの人、すごく酔っぱらってるね。壁にぶつかりそう。
B: **みっともない**ね。

A: That person looks really drunk. He almost bumped into the wall.
B: Not a pleasant sight.

❷ A day off

A: いつまでパジャマ着てるの、**みっともない**。
B: 休みだからいいじゃん。

A: Are you still in pajamas? Not a pleasant sight.
B: It's a day off. It's all right.

❸ A fight

A: 人前でけんかするなんて**みっともない**よ。
B: そうだね。反省してる。

A: It's disgraceful to fight in public.
B: Yes, I am sorry.

❹ Before a match

A: 練習、頑張ってるね。
B: うん。**みっともない**姿は見せられないからね。

A: You practice seriously.
B: Yes, I don't want to be seen as inadequate.

182 見（み）てられない *Miterarenai*

I can't bear to look

❁ **To be unable to look at something because to do so would cause one to worry or to be in pain.**

POINT
➡ (1) Used when worried about someone's words or actions.
　(2) Used when someone's appearance is pitiful.
　(3) Used when a performance or match is going poorly.

❶ When a poor cook is cooking.

A：代（か）わるよ！　怖（こわ）くて見（み）てられない！
B：え、そう？　じゃ、お願（ねが）い。

A: I'll do it for you! It's so scary I can't bear to watch you!
B: What, really? Then could you, please?

❷ Looking at a baby that just learned how to walk

A：おっと、危（あぶ）ない！
B：心配（しんぱい）で見（み）てられないね。

A: Whoa, watch out!
B: It's so worrying that you can't bear to look.

❸ Penalty kicks in a soccer match

A：ドキドキするね！
B：私（わたし）、もう見（み）てられない！

A: Doesn't it make your heart pound?
B: I can't bear to look!

❹ Watching TV

A：この子（こ）たち、かわいそうすぎる。
B：ほんとだよ。つらくて見（み）てられない。

A: Those poor, poor children.
B: Yes. It's so terrible I can't bear to watch.

197

183 見直した *Minaoshita*

Changed my opinion

❁ Indicates forming a more positive impression after having underestimated someone.

POINT
➡ Often implies surprise or admiration for some unexpected aspect.

---

❶ High score

A：この前の試験、90点でした。
B：へー、頑張ったじゃない。見直したよ。

A: I got 90% on the last test.
B: Wow, you must have really studied. I'm impressed.

❷ Cost of the lunch

A：部長が全員分おごってくれるなんて、驚いたね。
B：うん。ちょっと見直したよ。

A: What a surprise that the manager paid for everyone's meal.
B: Yeah. I see him in a new light.

❸ Hidden character

A：田中さんって、料理とか全然やらないと思ってた。見直したよ。
B：意外だよね。

A: I didn't think Tanaka-san cooked at all. I'm impressed.
B: That was unexpected.

❹ Unexpected remark

A：へー、彼がそんなこと言ったんだ。
B：ちょっと見直したでしょ？

A: Wow, so he really said that.
B: It changed your impression of him, didn't it?

184 難しいです *Muzukashii desu*

It's difficult. Not easy.

(1) This means that the chance of success is quite low, and the expectations of the other may not be met.
(2) It shows that something is too delicate to be dealt with.

POINT
> This is often used when you diplomatically convey a negative response.

❶ Repairing something

A: これを元に戻すんですか。ちょっと**難しいです**ね。
B: そうですか。

A: You need this repaired? Not an easy thing to do.
B: Isn't it?

❷ An invitation

A: 明日みんなでカラオケに行くんだけど、よかったら行かない？
B: 明日ですか。ちょっと**難しいです**ね。

A: We are all going to karaoke tomorrow. Why don't you come?
B: Tomorrow? That's a bit difficult.

❸ When in trouble

A: 人間関係ってなかなか**難しいです**ね。
B: そうだね。

A: Human relationships are difficult, aren't they?
B: True.

❹ About character

A: 森さんって、どんな人ですか。
B: ああ…。あの人はなかなか**難しいです**よ。

A: What kind of person is Mr. Mori?
B: Well, he is a rather difficult man.

185 無責任だなあ *Musekinin danaa*

How irresponsible

✿ Used to express feelings of unease or anger at someone's lack of feelings of responsibility.

POINT
➡ A strongly critical phrase.

---

❶ A break

A: 彼女は今日休みです。
B: え？ 会議があるのに？ しかも、今日は彼女のチームの発表だよ。**無責任だなあ**。

A: She took today off.
B: What? Even though we have a meeting? And it's her team's report, too. How irresponsible.

❷ An abandoned cat

A: ゴミ捨て場に子猫が捨てられてたんだって。
B: **無責任だなあ**。そういう人間は動物を飼う資格なんてないよ。

A: I heard that there was a kitten thrown away in the trash heap.
B: How irresponsible. People like that don't deserve to be able to keep pets.

❸ The actions of a ship captain

A: 船が沈みそうなのに、船長が先に逃げたんだって。
B: まじで!? **無責任だなあ**。

A: I heard that the captain went ahead and evacuated from the ship even though it was about to sink.
B: Seriously!? How irresponsible.

❹ An old model

A: メーカーに問い合わせたけど、古いモデルだから修理はだめだって。
B: **無責任だなあ**。じゃ、売らなきゃいいのに。

A: I contacted the manufacturer, but they said that they won't repair it because it's an old model.
B: How irresponsible. They shouldn't be selling it, then.

❺ Absent without permission

A: 田中さん、また無断で休んだの？ ほんとに**無責任だなあ**。
B: 困った人だね。

A: Tanaka-san took the day off without permission again? How irresponsible.
B: What a difficult person.

186 無茶です *Mucha desu*

That's impossible

❂ When things go too far, are done beyond reason, common sense or go over the limit.

POINT
➡ It includes a feeling of accusation about the reckless way things are being handled.

---

❶ Moderator

A：彼に司会をやらせるんですか。**無茶**ですよ。まだ新人なんだから。
B：そうか、難しいか。

A: Are you going to make him a moderator? That's not possible. He is still a newcomer.
B: Oh, you think it's difficult.

❷ Sales target

A：売り上げ目標、1000万円だって。
B：そんな、**無茶**だよ。

A: I heard that our sales goal will be 10 million yen.
B: That's impossible.

❸ Having a fever

A：えっ？ 熱あるのに試合に出るつもり？ **無茶**だよ。
B：大丈夫、大丈夫。

A: What? Are you going to play the game with a fever? That's impossible.
B: I will be all right.

❹ Home party

A：急なんだけど、明日、うちでホームパーティーできない？
B：えーっ？ そんな**無茶**なこと言わないでよ。

A: This is very sudden, but is it okay if we have a party at home tomorrow?
B: What? That's impossible.

187 無理しなくていい *Murishinakute ii*

You don't need to force yourself

✿ Expresses feelings that it is okay for someone to not force themselves to try to do something.

POINT
➡ Often used when someone is very busy or in poor health.

❶ When to submit

A：報告書は金曜日でもいいですか。
B：今忙しいんでしょ？ **無理しなくていい**よ。来週中にもらえれば。

A: Can I turn the report in on Friday?
B: Aren't you busy right now? You don't need to force yourself. As long as I can get it next week.

❷ Feeling unwell

A：顔色悪いよ。**無理しなくていい**から、帰ったら？
B：すみません。ありがとうございます。

A: You look pale. You don't need to force yourself, why don't you go home?
B: I'm sorry. Thank you.

❸ At a drinking party

A：あのう、私はお酒はあまり飲めないんです。
B：ああ、**無理しなくてもいい**よ。好きなの、飲んで。

A: Um, I can't drink very much alcohol.
B: Oh, no need to force yourself. Just drink however much you'd like.

❹ Plans

A：来週の金曜日ですか。うーん…。
B：難しいなら、**無理しなくていい**ですよ。

A: Friday next week? Hmm...
B: You don't need to force yourself if you can't.

❺ An invitation

A：来週の土曜、うちでバーベキューやるんだけど、よかったら来ない？ あ、でも、**無理しなくていい**からね。
B：あ、はい…。明日、お返事します。

A: We're going to have a barbecue at my home next Saturday. If you'd like, why don't you come? Oh, but you don't need to force yourself.
B: Oh, okay... I'll tell you tomorrow.

188 迷惑です *Meewaku desu*

What a nuisance. Feel annoyed.

❀ This is an expression to accuse the other when someone imposes on you.

POINT

➡ This is a strong caution to the other and so should be used only in extreme circumstances.

---

❶ Illegal parking

A：こんなところに自転車をとめて、**迷惑だ**なあ。
B：ほんと。

A: Someone has parked their bicycle here. What a nuisance.
B: True.

❷ At midnight, on the phone

A：こんな時間に電話して、**迷惑じゃ**なかった？
B：大丈夫だよ。起きてたから。

A: Are you annoyed with me phoning up this late?
B: It's all right. I was still awake.

❸ Someone who talks too much

A：あの人、親切なのはいいけど、説明がいつも長すぎる。
B：そうそう。ちょっと**迷惑なんだ**よね。

A: That man is kind, but always goes on when explaining things.
B: True. We always feel annoyed.

❹ Boasting about children

A：あの二人はいつも子どもの自慢話だよね。
B：そうそう。いい**迷惑だ**よね。

A: Those two are always boasting about their children.
B: Yes, it annoys me.

❺ Without permission

A：知らない間に勝手に写真を使われていたよ。
B：えー！**迷惑な**話。

A: Without permission someone used your photo.
B: What? That's too much.

189 めんどくさい *Mendokusai*

It's tiring. It's too much work.

✿ It shows a feeling that something is tedious and unpleasant to do.

POINT

➡ "*Mendokusai*" is a shortened expression of "*mendookusai*" which emphasizes troublesomeness ("*mendoo da*").

---

❶ At home

A：食器洗っておいてね。
B：えー、**めんどくさい**。

A: Wash the dishes.
B: Why, it's too much work.

❷ New Year's card

A：手書きは**めんどくさい**から、パソコンで作ろう。
B：そうだね。

A: Making hand-written cards is tiring, so let's make them with the computer.
B: That's a good idea.

❸ At the office

A：報告書作るの、**めんどくさい**なあ。
B：簡単なのでいいんじゃない？

A: Making this report is tiring.
B: A simple one is fine, I think.

❹ At home

A：雨やまないね。
B：うん。なんか、行くのが**めんどくさく**なってきた。

A: The rain doesn't stop.
B: No, I don't feel like going out. It's a nuisance.

190 もう限界 *Moo genkai*

I'm at my limit

❁ Used to express feelings that one cannot go any further

POINT
➡ Often used when being unable to endure something for any longer.

---

① At a marathon

A：だめだ、**もう限界**。これ以上走れない。
B：もうすぐゴールだから頑張って！

A: No, I'm at my limit. I can't run any farther.
B: You're almost at the goal, you can do it!

② Full

A：**もう限界**！　これ以上入らない。
B：無理して全部食べなくてもいいよ。

A: I'm at my limit! I'm completely full.
B: You don't need to force yourself to eat everything.

③ Lifespan of a computer

A：そのパソコン、10年も使ってるんだ。
B：うん。さすがに**もう限界**かな。いろいろ調子が悪くなってきたよ。

A: So you've been using that computer for ten years?
B: Yes, but maybe it's almost at its limit. It hasn't been acting well in a lot of ways.

④ On the phone

A：いつになったら来るの!?　**もう限界**だよ。
B：ごめんごめん。もうすぐ着くから。

A: (On the phone) When are you getting here!? I'm at my limit.
B: Sorry, sorry. I'll be there soon.

⑤ The workplace

A：**もう**我慢の**限界**。こんな会社、やめてやる！
B：どうしたの？

A: I can't take any more. I'm quitting this company!
B: What's the matter?

191 申し分ない *Mooshibun nai*

It's perfect

❖ An outcome or performance is excellent and there is no complaint or defect.

POINT
➡ This is often used when a superior gives their impression or evaluation. It's better not to use it to those of higher position.

---

❶ At a dining table

A：お味はいかがですか。
B：申し分ないです。

A: How does it taste?
B: It's perfect.

❷ At a shop

A：あのカメラはどう？
B：性能は申し分ないけど、ちょっと高いかな。

A: How is this camera?
B: Its performance is perfect, but it's a bit expensive.

❸ At a workplace

A：さすが、青木さん。申し分ない仕上がりです。
B：ありがとうございます。

A: I am proud of you, Ms. Aoki. It looks perfect.
B: Thank you very much.

❹ Access to the station

A：もうちょっと駅から近ければ申し分ないんだけどなあ。
B：ま、ぜいたくは言えないよ。

A: It would be perfect if it were a bit closer to the station.
B: But you won't find a better one than this.

192 もうだめだ *Moo dame da*

Can't keep going; (I'm) done

❀ Used to express feelings of being unable to maintain something for any longer.

POINT
➡ Used both about people and things.

---

① Hiking

A：**もうだめだ**、歩けない。ちょっと休もう？
B：そうだね。

A: I can't keep walking any further. Can we take a little break?
B: Sounds good.

② An old washer

A：この洗濯機、**もうだめだ**。
B：あーあ。とうとう壊れた？

A: This washer can't keep going.
B: Oh dear. So it finally broke?

③ Before a meal

A：**もうだめ**。待てない！ 食べてもいい？
B：少しだけだよ。

A: I'm done. I can't wait! Can I eat?
B: Just a little bit.

④ 10 more minutes

A：**もうだめだ**、間に合わない。
A：あと10分だからわからないよ。とりあえず走ろう。

A: We're done for, we won't make it.
B: It's only ten more minutes, we don't know. Let's just run.

207

193 もっともです *Mottomo desu*

I agree

❋ Used to express feelings of agreement when someone's words or actions are reasonable.

POINT
- A phrase used when constantly accepting someone's words and actions.
- *"Gomottomo desu"* is used to superiors.

---

① Advice

A: もう一度最初からやったほうがいいんじゃないですか。

B: そうですね、**もっともです**。

A: Wouldn't it be better for you to do this again from the beginning?

B: Yes, I agree.

② Why someone is mad

A: 誕生日、忘れちゃったの？ 彼女が怒るのも**もっともだ**よ。

B: そうだね。

A: You forgot her birthday? It makes sense for your girlfriend to be mad.

B: You're right.

③ At a store

A: お客様のおっしゃることは**ごもっともです**。スタッフによく注意しておきます。

B: たのみますよ。

A: I completely agree with what you say. I'll be sure to give a stern warning to my staff.

B: Please do.

Variations

④ Not that simple

A: それは**もっともな**意見だけど、言うほど簡単じゃないよ。

B: そうかなあ。

A: I agree with what you say, but it's not that simple.

B: I wonder.

194 物足りない *Monotarinai*

Lacking; insufficient

❖ **Used to express feelings of dissatisfaction and wanting more, or feelings that something is missing**

POINT
➡ Used when one has vague feelings of being dissatisfied despite not knowing why.

---

❶ At a restaurant

A: ごちそうさま。あー、お腹いっぱい。
B: そう？ 僕はまだ**物足りない**。

A: Thank you for the meal. Oh, I'm stuffed.
B: Really? That wasn't enough for me.

❷ At an amusement park

A: 結構いろいろ乗ったね。そろそろ帰る？
B: えー、まだ**物足りない**。あと３つくらい乗ろうよ。

A: We went on quite a lot of rides. Do you want to head back now?
B: What? I'm not satisfied yet. Let's go on three or so more.

❸ Playing a game

A: だめだ。僕の負けだ。
B: なんだ、もう終わり？ ちょっと**物足りない**なあ。

A: It's no good. I lose.
B: What, you're done already? I don't feel quite satisfied.

❹ A design sample

A: どう？ チラシのデザイン。
B: うーん、なんか**物足りない**なあ。赤で「新発売」とか入れる？

A: How is the flier's design?
B: Hm, it feels lacking. Why don't you add "New release" in red?

❺ A taste

A: スープを作ってみたんだけど、ちょっと食べてみて。
B: 悪くないけど、なんか**物足りない**気がする。塩を足してみたら？

A: I made this soup, can you try tasting it?
B: It's not bad, but it feels like it's lacking something. Why don't you try adding more salt?

195 やった *Yatta*

(I / We) did it

✿ Used to express feeling of joy when a job is completed or when a goal is reached.

POINT

➡ "*Yatta*" is used when talking about yourself, while "*Yatta ne.*" and "*Yoku yatta.*" are often used when talking about others.

❶ Finishing work

A: やったー、書類も全部完成。
B: お疲れ様。

A: I did it! I finished all the documents, too.
B: Good work.

❷ Winning a lottery

A: おっ、この前買った宝くじ、当たってるよ。
B: 本当？ やったね。

A: Hey, the lottery ticket I bought the other day was a winner.
B: Really? You did it!

❸ Passing

A: 先生、試験に合格しました。
B: おめでとう。よくやったよ。

A: Sensei, I passed the exam.
B: Good job. You did it.

❹ After a match is over

A: 負けちゃったね。あと、もうちょっとだったのに…。
B: うん。でも、よくやったよ。

A: So we lost. If we only tried a little harder…
B: Yeah. But you did a good job.

196 やっと一段落する

Yatto ichidanraku suru

Quiet down, finally able to take a breath

✿ To come to a resting place after a difficult job.

POINT
▶▶ Used when a situation quiets down after an extended busy period.

---

❶ Next week is OK

A：最近忙しくてなかなか会えないね。
B：やっと仕事が一段落したから、来週なら会えると思うよ。

A: You've been so busy lately that you haven't been able to meet.
B: My work finally quieted down, so I think I could meet you next week.

❷ After moving

A：引っ越しの荷物はもう片付いたんですか。
B：なかなか片付かなかったんですが、やっと一段落しました。

A: Did you clean up all of your things you moved?
B: It took a while to clean them up, but I'm finally at a resting point.

❸ Busy days

A：今の仕事が一段落したら、ちょっと休みをとったら？
B：そうだね。温泉でも行こうかな。

A: Would you like to take a break once you reach a resting place on your current job?
B: Yes, maybe I'll go to a hot spring.

❹ Completing an essay

A：やっと論文ができた！
B：お疲れ様。これでやっと一段落できるね。

A: My essay is finally done!
B: Good work. Now you can finally sit back and take a breath.

211

197 やめとく *Yametoku*

I'll pass; I'll hold off

❁ Used when making a decision to not do something because it will bring about a negative result.

POINT
➡ *"Yametoku"* is a shortening of *"yameteoku."*

---

❶ At a pub

A：もう一軒どう？
B：いや、明日も早いから**やめとく**よ。

A: How about going to one more store?
B: No, I need to be up early tomorrow. I'll pass.

Variations

❷ When sick

A：まだ熱があるんだから、外出は**やめといたら？**
B：そうだね。

A: You still have a fever, so why don't you hold off on going outside?
B: You're right.

❸ A warning

A：株でもやって儲けようかな。
B：**やめといたほうがいい**よ。大損するかもしれないよ。

A: Maybe I should get into stocks to make some money.
B: You should pass. You could lose a ton.

❹ Regret

A：あの件、部長に言ったの？
B：うん…。でも、**やめとけばよかった**。逆に、いろいろ注意されたよ。

A: Did you talk to the division chief about that thing?
B: Yeah... But I should have passed. He actually gave me a lot of warnings instead.

198 やるしかない *Yaru shika nai*

Have to do it

✿ Used to express feelings of resignation and resolution when there is no choice but to do something.

POINT

➡ Often used as a term of encouragement along with expressing the resolution that one has to do something.

❶ After coming this far

A：もうやめとく？
B：ここまできたら、**やるしかない**よ。

A: Do you want to quit?
B: We have to do it after we came this far.

❷ It's work

A：あー、めんどくさいな。
B：仕事なんだから**やるしかない**でしょ。

A: Oh, what a pain.
B: It's work, you have to do it.

❸ Something needed

A：どうせ**やるしかない**なら、早く終わらせよう。
B：そうだね。

A: If we have to do it anyway, let's get it over with.
B: You're right.

❹ Can't be helped

A：**やるしかない**のはわかってるけど、どうもやる気が出ないんだ。
B：そういう時もあるよね。

A: I know I have to do it, but I just can't get in the mood to.
B: There are times like that.

199 やるね *Yaru ne*

Nice job

❋ An expression used to recognize and praise someone's abilities.

POINT
➡ "*Yaru*" means "to do something in an impressive way" and "to use one's strength," and expresses feelings of admiration.

---

❶ Successfully bargaining

A: このパン、100円にしてもらったよ。
B: **やるね**。

A: I got him to sell me this bread for 100 yen.
B: Nice job.

❷ Hand-made

A: 今日、ケーキ作ったよ。
B: おっ、**やるなあ**。

A: I made this cake today.
B: Wow, nice job.

❸ At an office

A: さっきのプレゼン、よかったよ。なかなか**やるねー**。
B: ありがとうございます。

A: That presentation just now was good. Pretty nice job there.
B: Thank you.

❹ Not losing to the cold

A: 冬も毎朝走ってるよ。
B: 寒いのによく**やるねー**。

A: I run every morning, in the winter, too.
B: Even in the cold? Nice job.

200 やればできる *Yarebadekiru*

You can do it if you try

❖ That one has the qualities needed to succeed at something if they put in effort.

POINT
➡ Often used with a sense that someone could succeed at something with effort, but that they are not giving it enough effort.

---

❶ Encouragement

A：私には才能ないのかなあ。
B：そんなことないよ。**やればできる**んだから、自信持って。

A: Maybe I'm just talentless.
B: That's not true. You can do it if you try, so have some confidence.

❷ Inexperienced

A：え？ スキー滑れないの？
B：というか、やったことがないから。**やればできる**よ。

A: Huh? You can't ski?
B: Well, it's that I've never tried. I can do it if I try.

❸ Not enough effort

A：**やればできる**のに…。もったいないなあ。
B：努力が足りないんですね。頑張ります。

A: You can do it if you just try... What a waste.
B: So my problem is that I'm not trying hard enough? I'll do my best, then.

❹ Proof

A：ね、私の言ったとおりでしょ。
B：そうですね。**やればできる**もんですね。

A: See? It's just like I said.
B: You're right. I can do it if I try.

❺ Passing

A：やっと合格しました！
B：なんだ、**やればできる**じゃん！

A: I finally passed!
B: Wow, so you can do it if you try!

201 許せない　*Yurusenai*

Unforgivable

✿ Used to express strong feelings of criticism by scolding an awful action as "something that ought not to be done."

POINT
➡ Often used to describe socially or morally forbidden acts or acts that injure the feelings of others.

---

❶ Breaking social rules

A：こんなところにごみを捨てるなんて、ひどいなあ。

B：きれいな景色が台無し。**許せない**！

A: It's awful that someone would throw their garbage out here.
B: They've ruined this beautiful scene. Unforgivable!

❷ Will you apologize?

A：彼もあんなに謝ってるんだから、許してあげたら？

B：無理、無理。絶対に**許せない**！

A: Why don't you forgive him? He's apologized so much.
B: No, no! I'll never forgive him!

❸ Animal abuse

A：動物をいじめるなんて**許せない**！　最低の人間だよ。

B：ほんとだよねえ。

A: It's unforgivable to bully animals! Only the worst kind of person would do that.
B: You're absolutely right.

❹ An awful thing to say

A：そんなひどいことを言ったの？　それは**許せない**ね。

B：でしょう？

A: He said something that awful? That's unforgivable.
B: Isn't it?

❺ Being robbed

A：かばんを盗まれたんだって？

B：そう。大事なものがいっぱい入ってったのに。もう**許せない**！

A: Someone stole your bag?
B: Yes. It was full of important things, too. It's unforgivable!

216

202 よくあること *Yoku aru koto*

That happens often. It's nothing unusual.

❁ It happens everyday and is nothing unusual.

POINT
➡ This is used when you console someone who has failed at something or suffered misfortune.

---

❶ About greetings

A：あいさつを無視されるって、ほんと気分悪いよね。
B：**よくあること**だよ。

A: Isn't it unpleasant when someone ignores your greeting.
B: That happens often.

❷ At a popular restaurant

A：えっ、１時間待ち!?
B：ああ、**よくあること**だよ。ここ、人気あるから。

A: What? We have to wait for two hours?!
B: Yeah, it's nothing unusual. This restaurant is popular.

❸ Oversleeping

A：せっかくの休日なのに、起きたらもうお昼…。
B：**よくあること**だよ。ぼくなんか、しょっちゅう。

A: It was a day off, and it was already noon when I woke up.
B: That happens often. It happens to me all the time.

❹ Getting on the wrong train

A：ぎりぎり間に合ったと思ったら、逆方向だったよ。もう、がっくり。
B：**よくあること**だよ。

A: I was about to rush onto the train but found it was headed in the opposite direction. Damn.
B: It's nothing unusual.

203 よく言うよ *Yoku iu yo*

You're one to talk; Are you kidding?

❖ Indicates an appalled, critical reaction to someone's preposterous remark.

POINT
➡ Often used about people who criticize others without reflecting on their own faults.

❶ At a school

A: マイケルは授業サボりすぎだよ。
B: **よく言うよ**。自分だってそうでしょ？

A: Michael skips class too often.
B: You're one to talk. Aren't you just the same?

❷ Crybaby

A: 私、すぐ泣く女の人って苦手。
B: **よく言うよ**。自分もかなりの泣き虫じゃない。

A: I don't like women who are quick to burst into tears.
B: Look who's talking. You're quite a crybaby yourself.

❸ A reply to an e-mail

A: なんでメールの返事くれないの！
B: **よく言うよ**。自分だって返事しないことが多いのに。

A: Why don't you answer my email?
B: Are you kidding? You also frequently fail to respond to emails.

❹ A man who quit smoking recently

A: だめだよ、ここで吸ったら！ 今月から禁煙になったんだから。
B: **よく言うよ**。この間まで吸ってたくせに。

A: No, you can't smoke here! It's a no-smoking area as of this month.
B: You're one to talk. You were smoking yourself until not long ago.

❺ Criticism of others

A: 部長にまた文句言われたよ。みんな頭が固いって。
B: **よく言うよ**ね。自分はどうなんだって。

A: The manager criticized me again. He said we were all stubborn.
B: Is he kidding? He ought to look at himself.

204 読めない *Yomenai*

Hard to read

❋ **Indicates that you can't infer a hidden meaning or future outcome based on the present situation.**

POINT

➡ "*Yomenai*" is often used to describe "*saki ga* ~ (about the future)", "*tenkai ga* ~ (about the outcome), " "*jookyoo ga* ~ (about the situation)", or "*kuuki ga* ~ (about the atmosphere)".

➡ However, it is also frequently used alone, omitting the subject.

❶ Prediction

A：今回はどこが優勝しそう？
B：うーん、ちょっとまだ**読めない**なあ。

A: Which team is likely to win this time?
B: Hmm, it's still sort of hard to say.

❷ About a colleague

A：彼は変わってるね。
B：うん…。ちょっと行動が**読めない**んだよね。

A: He's odd, isn't he.
B: Well, it's hard to interpret his behavior.

❸ In a bus

A：10時に間に合いそうですか。
B：ちょっと渋滞してるので、**読めない**ですね。

A: Do you think you can make it by 10:00?
B: Traffic is a little backed up, so it's hard to say.

❹ About visitors

A：明日、何人ぐらい来るかなあ。
B：天気にもよるし、**読めない**ね。

A: About how many people will come tomorrow?
B: It depends on the weather, so it's hard to predict.

219

205 余裕がある *Yoyuu ga aru*

Can afford to

✿ To have physical (economical, time-related) or mental freedom and to be calm and collected as a result.

POINT
➤ More conversational than "*yutori ga aru*" and frequently used in daily conversation.

---

❶ An impression

A: リサさんはいつも**余裕がある**ね。

B: えっ？ そんなことないですよ。そう見えるだけですよ。

A: You always have so much composure, Lisa-san.

B: What? That's not true, it just looks like that.

❷ At the workplace

A: 田中さん、今、**余裕ある**？

B: うん、ちょっとはね。何？

A: Do you have some time right now, Tanaka-san?

B: Yes, a little bit. What is it?

Variations

❸ At an art museum

A: **余裕があったら**、特別展示もご覧ください。

B: わかりました。

A: If you have the time, please visit the special exhibit as well.

B: I understand.

❹ An invitation

A: 一泊でキャンプに行く話があるんだけど、どう？

B: ああ…。**余裕があった**ら行きたいけど…。今はちょっと無理。

A: People are talking about going camping for a night, what do you think?

B: Oh, yeah... I'd like to go if I could afford to, but... I can't right now.

Related phrases

❺ 「余裕ですね」

A: もうできたんですか。**余裕ですね**。

B: そんなことないですよ。

A: So you're already done? That must have been easy for you.

B: That's not true.

206 余裕がない *Yoyuu ga nai*

Can't afford to

❁ To not have physical (economical, time-related) or mental room and to be unable to relax as a result.

POINT
▶ Its antonym is *"yoyuu ga aru."*

---

❶ Too busy

A：ちょっと手伝ってくれない？
B：ごめん、今、ちょっと**余裕がない**。

A: Could you help me out a little?
B: Sorry, I don't have the room to right now.

❷ Having no time

A：5時まであと1時間半くらいか…。**余裕ない**ね。
B：うん。ちょっと厳しいね。

A: An hour and a half until 5... There's no room to work with.
B: Yes. It's a bit tough.

❸ Invitation

A：金曜に飲み会があるんだけど、行かない？
B：ごめん。今月ちょっと**余裕ない**からやめとくよ。

A: We're going drinking on Friday, would you like to come?
B: Sorry, I don't have the room to this month.

❹ Suitcase

A：もっと入ると思ってたけど、全然**余裕ない**なあ。
B：そうか。じゃ、これは入らないね。

A: I thought more would fit, but there's no space at all.
B: I see. Then I guess this won't fit.

207 わかる Wakaru

I know; I understand

❋ Indicates understanding and sympathy for the other person's feelings.

POINT
➡ Sometimes repeated for emphasis: "*wakaru, wakaru.*"

❶ Hating oneself

A：ときどき自分が嫌になるよ。
B：わかるよ。私もそうだから。

A: Sometimes I can't stand myself.
B: I know. I'm the same.

❷ Getting sleepy

A：勉強しなきゃって思うんだけど、眠くなっちゃうんだよね。
B：わかるー！ 教科書開くと眠くなるよね。

A: I tell myself I have to study, but I get so sleepy.
B: I know! I get sleepy as soon as I open the textbook.

❸ Won't get out of my hair

A：最近、あのコマーシャルでかかってる曲が頭の中をぐるぐる回るんだよ。
B：わかる！ あの曲、おもしろいからね。

A: The song from that commercial has been stuck in my head lately.
B: I get it. That song is catchy.

❹ The reason for losing a game

A：どうしても、自分のせいで負けたって思っちゃう。
B：わかるよ。そう思うのはしょうがないと思う。

A: I can't help feeling that it was my fault we lost.
B: I know. I don't think there's any way to avoid feeling that way.

❺ Want to eat meay

A：疲れがたまってるからかなあ。今日はお肉が食べたい気分。
B：わかるわかる！ じゃ、ステーキ食べに行こう。

A: Maybe it's because I have so much accumulated fatigue. I feel like eating meat today.
B: Yeah, I know! Let's go out for steak.

208 わざとらしい *Wazatorashii*

Seems contrived. Sounds fake or insincere.

❁ The behavior is unnatural, contrived, without sincerity.

POINT

➡ This is used when you criticize the behavior of others or reflect on your own behavior.

❶ On the phone

A：(咳をして) ごめん。風邪ひいちゃって、今日は無理。
B：またー。咳が**わざとらしい**よ。

A: [Coughing] Sorry, I've got a cold and cannot come today.
B: Is it true? Your cough sounds fake.

❷ About a candidate

A：あの人、選挙の前だけいい人ぶるよね。
B：そう。なんか笑顔が**わざとらしい**。

A: That person pretends to be nice only before the election.
B: True. The smile seems rather fake.

❸ About what one says

A：さっきの私の言い方、ちょっと**わざとらしかった**？
B：え？ そんなことないんじゃない？

A: Did my expression sound a bit insincere?
B: Why? I don't think so.

❹ Surprising someone from behind

A：わあーっ、びっくりした！
B：うそー、気づいてたでしょう？ 今の、**わざとらしかった**よ。

A: Wow, you scared me!
B: Did I? I thought you knew it was me. Your reaction looks contrived.

209 悪いね（感謝の気持ち）
Warui ne

Sorry; my bad (meaning thanks)

❖ A phrase that conveys a sense of gratitude, along with feeling sorry for having caused trouble or a burden.

POINT
➡ Like "*sumimasen*," its basic meaning is an apology, but it also includes a sense of acknowledgment that "I made you do something for me."

❶ Submission

A：レポート、田中さんのも一緒に出してこようか。
B：そう？ 悪いね。

A: Shall I hand in your report together with mine, Tanaka-san?
B: Really? Thanks.

❷ A coffee break

A：ちょっと休んだら？ コーヒーいれたよ。
B：おお、悪いね。

A: Why not take a break? I made coffee.
B: Oh, thanks.

❸ A sudden rain

A：どうぞ、この傘を使ってください。
B：ああ、悪いね。

A: Here, please use this umbrella.
B: Oh, thanks.

❹ In a car

A：じゃ、途中まで送るよ。
B：いつも悪いですね。

A: I'll drive you part of the way.
B: You are always so kind.

❺ About the details

A：じゃ、詳細が決まったらメールするね。
B：ああ、悪い。

A: I'll email you when the details are finalized.
B: OK, thanks.

210 悪いね（謝罪の気持ち）
Waruine

Sorry; my bad (meaning an apology)

❖ Indicates feeling sorry and apologizing to someone.

POINT
➡ "*Warukatta (ne/yo/na)*" can be used sarcastically ("well, excuuuse me!") by stressing the final *ne*, *yo*, or *na*.

---

❶ On the phone

A：こんな夜中に悪いね。
B：いいけど、何？

A: I'm sorry to call you so late at night.
B: That's OK. What is it?

❷ On the phone

A：出席できなくて悪いね。
B：ううん、気にしないで。

A: I'm sorry that I won't be able to attend.
B: Don't worry about it.

❸ At the porch

A：わざわざ来てもらって悪いですね。
B：いいえ。

A: Thank you for coming all this way just for me.
B: Don't mention it.

❹ To a friend

A：昨日は急に行けなくなって悪かったね。
B：ううん。仕事、大丈夫だった？

A: I'm sorry that something came up at the last minute yesterday and I couldn't go.
B: That's all right. Was everything OK at your job?

❺ To a friend

A：あの時は、ひどいことを言って、本当に悪かった。
B：もういいよ。気にしてないから。

A: I am very sorry that I said such an awful thing that time.
B: Forget it. I don't hold it against you.

❻ Watching a TV program

A：へー、家庭でもあんな料理が簡単にできるんだ。
B：大した料理ができなくて悪かったね！

A: I never knew dishes like that could be easily prepared at home.
B: Well, excuse me for not being a gourmet chef!

225

さくいん（英語）　INDEX (English)

A

- A big dea　たいしたもんだ …………… 132
- Absurd　ばかばかしい ……………… 170
- Accept (your) kind offer
  おことばにあまえて ……………… 46
- Accordingly　それなりに …………… 117
- Again?　また― ……………………… 188
- Ahead of you　おさきに …………… 47
- All or nothing　いちかばちか ……… 33
- Am I bothering you
  ごめいわくじゃないですか …………… 93
- Anyway　それはそうと ……………… 120
- Are you kidding?　よくいうよ ……… 218
- As it is　それなりに ………………… 117
- (Not) ~at all　ぜんぜん ……………… 109
- At any rate　いちおう ……………… 32

B

- Be annoyed with　カチンとくる ……… 55
- Be more clear　はっきりして ………… 173
- Boring　うんざり ……………………… 44
- Bothers me　きになる ………………… 76
- Bummed out　がっくり ……………… 56
- Burned out　がっくり ………………… 56

C

- Can afford to　よゆうがある ………… 220
- Can you believe it?　ひどくない? …… 176
- Can't keep going　もうだめだ ……… 207
- Can't afford to　よゆうがない ……… 221
- Can't bear　たえられない …………… 133
- Can't you (please) make it work
  そこをなんとか（おねがいします） …… 112
- Changed my opinion　みなおした …… 198
- Come on　まったく …………………… 193
- Counting on you　たよりにしてます … 136
- Cut it out　いいかげんにして ………… 25

D

- Depend on you　たよりにしてます …… 136
- Depressed　おちこむ ………………… 49
- Depressing　へこむ …………………… 179
- (I / We) did it　やった ……………… 210
- Did something happen?
  なんかあったの? …………………… 164
- Difficult　つらい ……………………… 141
- Doesn't seem right　なっとくいかない 156
- (I'm) done　もうだめだ ……………… 207
- Don't brood over　くよくよしないで … 87
- Don't care a bit　どうでもいい ……… 145
- Don't fret over　くよくよしないで …… 87
- Don't give a damn　どうでもいい …… 145
- Don't rush me so much
  そんなに（あんまり）せかさないで …… 126
- Don't worry about　くよくよしないで … 87
- Don't worry about ~　ほっとく ……… 183
- Don't you agree?
  そうおもわない? …………………… 111
- Don't you think so?
  そうおもわない? …………………… 111
- Down　おちこむ ……………………… 49
- Down in the dumps　がっくり ……… 56

E

- Easygoing　きらくに …………………… 84
- Exactly as you say
  おっしゃるとおりです ……………… 50

F

- Feel annoyed　めいわくです ………… 203
- Feel bad　きもちわるい ……………… 80
- Feel depressed　へこむ ……………… 179
- Feel depressed　きがおもい ………… 66
- Feel down　きがおもい ……………… 66
- Feel sick　きもちわるい ……………… 80

Index (English)

Feel so good　きもちいい ･･････････････ 79
Finally able to take a breath
　　やっといちだんらくする ･･････････････ 211
For Christ's sake　まったく ････････････ 193
For now　いちおう ･･････････････････････ 32

G
Get on one's nerves　カチンとくる ････ 55
Getting better　ぼちぼち ･･･････････････ 182
Give me a break　かんべんして ･･･････ 64
Going well　うまくいってる ･････････････ 43
Great　えらい ･･････････････････････････ 45

H
Happy-go-lucky　きらくに ･･････････････ 84
Hard to accept　なっとくがいかない ････ 156
Hard to believe　いがい ････････････････ 31
Hard to read　よめない ････････････････ 219
Hasn't changed　かわらないです ･･･････ 60
Have no motivation　ちからがでない ･･ 138
Have no strength　ちからがでない ･････ 138
Have to do it　やるしかない ････････････ 213
How are you doing?
　　ちょうしはどう？ ･･････････････････････ 139
How are you?　ぐあいはどう？ ･･･････････ 86
How can that be?　そんなばかな ･･････ 127
How do I put it　なんていったらいいか ･･ 166
How do you feel?　ぐあいはどう？ ･･････ 86
How irresponsible　むせきにんだなあ ･･ 200
How is it coming along?
　　ちょうしはどう？ ･･････････････････････ 139
How rude　しつれいだなあ ･････････････ 101
How sharp　するどいなあ ･･････････････ 108
How stylish　おしゃれですね ･･･････････ 48
How thoughtful　きがきくね ････････････ 67
How?　どうやって？ ･･････････････････ 147

I
I agree　どうかんです ･･････････････････ 142
I agree　もっともです ･･････････････････ 208
I apologize for suddenly bringing this up
　　きゅうなはなしできょうしゅくですが ･･････ 81
I can't bear to look　みてられない ････ 197
I can't believe it　なんてことだ ･･････････ 167
I can't choose　なやむ ････････････････ 163
I can't decide　なやむ ･････････････････ 163
I can't do it　まねできない ･････････････ 194
I can't let that happen
　　そういうわけにはいかない ･･････････････ 110
(I / We) did it　やった ････････････････ 210
I don't get it　なんだかなあ ･･････････ 165
I don't have a clue
　　さっぱりわからない ････････････････････ 99
I don't know what to say
　　なんていったらいいか ･･･････････････ 166
I don't know what to say
　　なんともいえない ･････････････････････ 169
I don't understand (what you mean)
　　いみがわからない ････････････････････ 38
I don't want to　いやだ ･･････････････ 39
I envy you　いいな ･･････････････････ 27
I got flustered　あせる ･･･････････････ 17
I had my hopes up
　　きたいしてたんだけど ･････････････････ 72
I hope nothing happens
　　なにもなければいいけど ･･････････････ 159
I knew it　だよね ･･･････････････････ 135
I know　わかる ････････････････････ 222
I never heard about that　きいてない ･･ 65
I sympathize　どうじょうするよ ････････ 143
I thought so　だよね ･･･････････････ 135
I told you　だからいったのに ･･････････ 134
I understand　わかる ･･･････････････ 222
I was being careless　うっかりしてた ･･ 41

227

さくいん（英語）

I will contact you later
　おってごれんらくします・・・・・・・・・・・・・・・・・ 51
I'm ashamed　はずかしい ・・・・・・・・・・・・・・ 172
I'm disgusted　あきれる ・・・・・・・・・・・・・・・・ 16
(I'm) done　もうだめだ ・・・・・・・・・・・・・・・・・ 207
I'm dumbfounded　あきれる ・・・・・・・・・・ 16
I'm impressed　かんしんする ・・・・・・・・・・・ 63
I'm impressed　なかなか ・・・・・・・・・・・・・・ 153
I'm leaving it to you　まかせた ・・・・・・・・ 187
If it's all right　おことばにあまえて ・・・・・・・ 46
I'll hold off　やめとく ・・・・・・・・・・・・・・・・・・ 212
I'll pass　やめとく ・・・・・・・・・・・・・・・・・・・・ 212
I'm at my limit　もうげんかい ・・・・・・・・・・ 205
I'm glad it worked out
　それはよかった ・・・・・・・・・・・・・・・・・・・・・ 122
I'm relieved　ほっとしました ・・・・・・・・・・・ 184
I'm relieved to hear that
　それをきいてあんしんした ・・・・・・・・・・・ 124
I'm sorry for my selfish request
　かってをいってすみません ・・・・・・・・・・・・ 59
I'm sorry if I'm mistaken
　まちがってたらごめん ・・・・・・・・・・・・・・・ 192
(Your / my) imagination　きのせい ・・・・・ 77
Impressive　たいしたもんだ ・・・・・・・・・・・ 132
In its own way　それなりに ・・・・・・・・・・・ 117
In that case　それじゃ ・・・・・・・・・・・・・・・ 114
Indebted to　おんにきる ・・・・・・・・・・・・・・ 54
Insufficient　ものたりない ・・・・・・・・・・・・ 209
Interested in　きになる ・・・・・・・・・・・・・・・ 76
Is it any surprise?
　こんなもんじゃない? ・・・・・・・・・・・・・・・・ 96
Is that so?　そっか ・・・・・・・・・・・・・・・・・ 113
Is this okay?　これでいい? ・・・・・・・・・・・・ 94
Isn't it awful?　ひどくない? ・・・・・・・・・・・ 176
Isn't that (about) what you'd expect?
　こんなもんじゃない? ・・・・・・・・・・・・・・・・ 96

It almost killed me　しぬほど ・・・・・・・・・ 102
It can't be so　そんなはずはない ・・・・・・ 128
It doesn't matter　かんけいない ・・・・・・・ 62
It is hard to say, but
　いいにくいんですが ・・・・・・・・・・・・・・・・・ 28
It makes me want to cry
　なきたくなる ・・・・・・・・・・・・・・・・・・・・・・ 154
It was over in the blink of an eye
　あっというま ・・・・・・・・・・・・・・・・・・・・・・・ 19
It will do　とくにもんだいない ・・・・・・・・・ 150
It's difficult　むずかしいです ・・・・・・・・・・ 199
It's embarrassing　はずかしい ・・・・・・・・ 172
It's hard to explain　うまくいえない ・・・・・ 42
It's in line　いいせんいってる ・・・・・・・・・・ 26
It's instructive　べんきょうになる ・・・・・・ 181
(It's) only getting started
　まだまだこれからです ・・・・・・・・・・・・・・・ 191
It's painful　それはいたい ・・・・・・・・・・・・ 118
It's perfect　もうしぶんない ・・・・・・・・・・・ 206
It's tiring　めんどくさい ・・・・・・・・・・・・・・・ 204
It's too much work　めんどくさい ・・・・・・ 204
It's amazing　さいこう ・・・・・・・・・・・・・・・・ 97
It's no big deal　たいしたことない ・・・・・・ 131
It's not like I'm mad
　べつにおこってない ・・・・・・・・・・・・・・・・ 180
It's nothing　それほどでもないです ・・・・・ 123
It's nothing　なんでもない ・・・・・・・・・・・・ 168
It's nothing special
　たいしたことない ・・・・・・・・・・・・・・・・・・ 131
It's nothing unusual　よくあること ・・・・ 217
It's rough　きついです ・・・・・・・・・・・・・・・・ 73
It's the best　さいこう ・・・・・・・・・・・・・・・・ 97
It's tight　きついです ・・・・・・・・・・・・・・・・・ 73

J

Just a step away　あといっぽ ・・・・・・・・・・ 20
Just as I thought　おもったとおり ・・・・・・・ 53

Index (English)

Just between you and me
    ここだけのはなしですが 90

L

Lacking　いまひとつ 37
Lacking　ものたりない 209
Lame　かっこわるい 57
Leave ~ alone　ほっとく 183
Let me think it over　けんとうします 88
Let's do it another time
    またにしよう 190
Let's try again another time
    またがんばろう 189
Let's stop here for today
    きょうはここまでにしましょう 83
Let's wait and see
    しばらくようすをみましょう 103
~ like it　きにいった 74
Lost respect　みそこなった 195
~ love it　きにいった 74

M

Marvelous　すばらしい 106
Misjudged　みそこなった 195
Moving on　それはそうと 120
My bad (meaning an apology)
    わるかった 225
My bad (meaning thanks)
    わるいね 224

N

Neither is better than the other
    どっちもどっちだ 151
Nice job　やるね 214
No　ちがう 137
No big deal　どうってことない 144
No need for an excuse
    いいわけはいい 29

No one else can do it　まねできない ... 194
No way　それはないよ 121
Not a pleasant sight　みっともない 196
Not bad　なかなか 153
Not easy　むずかしいです 199
Not fair　ずるい 107
(Not) ~at all　ぜんぜん 109
Not in the mood　きがすすまない 69
Not really　それほどでもないです 123
Not really　とくにない／とくには 149
Not so serious　きらくに 84
Not too bad　ぼちぼち 182
Not totally　いまひとつ 37
Not what I've heard　はなしがちがう .. 175
Nothing in particular
    とくにない／とくには 149
Nothing to say　ことばもでない 91
Nothing to worry about
    どうってことない 144
Nothing unusual　あたりまえです 18

O

Obviously　あたりまえです 18
Of course　あたりまえです 18
Of course　きまってる 78
Of course　それはそうだ 119
Oh you　また— 188
(It's) only getting started
    まだまだこれからです 191
Out of the question　ありえない 22

P

Pissed off　カチンとくる 55
Pitiful　なさけない 155
Please do it as soon as possible
    しきゅう、おねがいします 100

229

さくいん（英語）

Please do it right away
　しきゅう、おねがいします・・・・・・・・・・・・・・・・・ 100
Pointless　ばかばかしい・・・・・・・・・・・・・・・・・ 170
Pretend you didn't hear that
　きかなかったことにして・・・・・・・・・・・・・・・・・・・ 70
Putting that aside　それはそうと・・・・・・・ 120

Q
Quiet down　やっといちだんらくする・・・・ 211

R
Really　それほどでもないです・・・・・・・・・・・・・ 123
Rely on you　たよりにしてます・・・・・・・・・ 136
Rough　つらい・・・・・・・・・・・・・・・・・・・・・・・・・・・・・・・・ 141

S
(To) say too much　ひとことおおい・・・・ 178
Scandalized　あきれる・・・・・・・・・・・・・・・・・・・・ 16
Seems contrived　わざとらしい・・・・・・・・ 223
Seriously?　なによ／なんだよ・・・・・・・・・・・・ 161
Sink or swim　いちかばちか・・・・・・・・・・・・・・ 33
So that's why　それでか・・・・・・・・・・・・・・・・・・ 115
Something like that
　そんなかんじです・・・・・・・・・・・・・・・・・・・・・・・・・・ 125
Sorry　わるいね・・・・・・・・・・・・・・・・・・・・・・・・・・・ 224
Sorry　わるかった・・・・・・・・・・・・・・・・・・・・・・・・ 225
Sorry for the trouble
　おてすうをおかけします・・・・・・・・・・・・・・・・・・・ 52
Sorry if I rubbed you the wrong way
　きにさわったらごめん・・・・・・・・・・・・・・・・・・・・・ 75
Sounds fake or insincere
　わざとらしい・・・・・・・・・・・・・・・・・・・・・・・・・・・・・・ 223
Splendid　すばらしい・・・・・・・・・・・・・・・・・・・・・ 106
Such nonsense　そんなばかな・・・・・・・・・・ 127
Surprisingly　いがい・・・・・・・・・・・・・・・・・・・・・・・・ 31

T
Take it easy　きらくに・・・・・・・・・・・・・・・・・・・・・ 84

Take it easy　ほどほどにね・・・・・・・・・・・・・・・ 185
Tell me whenever
　いつでもいってください・・・・・・・・・・・・・・・・・・ 35
Tentative　いちおう・・・・・・・・・・・・・・・・・・・・・・・・ 32
That happens often　よくあること・・・・ 217
That hurts　それはいたい・・・・・・・・・・・・・・・ 118
That makes sense　どうりで・・・・・・・・・・・・ 148
That seems ridiculous　ばかみたい・・・・ 171
That sounds fishy　あやしい・・・・・・・・・・・・ 21
That's awful　それはいたい・・・・・・・・・・・・・ 118
That's impossible　むちゃです・・・・・・・・・ 201
That's wrong　ちがう・・・・・・・・・・・・・・・・・・・・・ 137
That's good news　それはよかった・・・・・ 122
That's how it is　そんなもんだよ・・・・・・・・ 130
The first I've heard of it
　はつみみです・・・・・・・・・・・・・・・・・・・・・・・・・・・・・・ 174
The same (as always)
　かわらないです・・・・・・・・・・・・・・・・・・・・・・・・・・・・ 60
The worst　さいてい・・・・・・・・・・・・・・・・・・・・・・・ 98
There are days like that
　そんなひもあるよ・・・・・・・・・・・・・・・・・・・・・・・・・ 129
There aren't many chances like this
　こんなチャンスはめったにない・・・・・・・・・・・ 95
There's no taking that back
　とりかえしがつかない・・・・・・・・・・・・・・・・・・・・ 152
There's no end to it　きりがない・・・・・・・・ 85
There's no particular problem
　とくにもんだいないです・・・・・・・・・・・・・・・・・ 150
There's nothing I can say
　なんともいえない・・・・・・・・・・・・・・・・・・・・・・・・・ 169
This is normal　いつものこと・・・・・・・・・・・・ 36
This isn't someone else's problem
　ひとごとじゃない・・・・・・・・・・・・・・・・・・・・・・・・・ 177
This isn't the time for that
　それどころじゃない・・・・・・・・・・・・・・・・・・・・・・ 116
This stays here
　ここだけのはなしですが・・・・・・・・・・・・・・・・・・ 90

Index (English)

Ticked off　イライラする ・・・・・・・・・・・・・・・ 40
Tiresome　うんざり ・・・・・・・・・・・・・・・・・・・・・・ 44
To death　しぬほど ・・・・・・・・・・・・・・・・・・・・ 102
(To) say too much　ひとことおおい ・・・・ 178
Tough　つらい ・・・・・・・・・・・・・・・・・・・・・・・・ 141
Tthat's what I said　だからいったのに ・・ 134

U

Uncool　かっこわるい ・・・・・・・・・・・・・・・・・・ 57
Unforgivable　ゆるせない ・・・・・・・・・・・・・ 216
Unpleasant　きもちわるい ・・・・・・・・・・・・・・ 80
Unreasonable　それはないよ ・・・・・・・・・・ 121
Unthinkable　かんがえられない ・・・・・・・・ 61
Usual (thing)　いつものこと ・・・・・・・・・・・・ 36

W

Was on pins and needles
　　きがきじゃなかった ・・・・・・・・・・・・・・・・・・ 68
Weak　ちからがでない ・・・・・・・・・・・・・・・ 138
Well then　それじゃ ・・・・・・・・・・・・・・・・・・ 114
What a nuisance　めいわくです ・・・・・・・ 203
What are you doing?
　　なにやってるの？ ・・・・・・・・・・・・・・・・・・・ 160
What are you thinking?
　　なにをかんがえてるんですか ・・・・・・・・・・ 162
What are you trying to say?
　　なにがいいたいの？ ・・・・・・・・・・・・・・・・・ 158
What are you up to?
　　なにやってるの？ ・・・・・・・・・・・・・・・・・・・ 160
What did I tell you?
　　だからいったのに ・・・・・・・・・・・・・・・・・・・ 134
What is it?　なに？ ・・・・・・・・・・・・・・・・・ 157
What is it?　なによ／なんだよ ・・・・・・・・ 161
What should I say
　　なんていったらいいか ・・・・・・・・・・・・・・・ 166
What's going on?　どうなってる？ ・・・・・ 146
What's happening?　どうなってる？ ・・・ 146

What's this all about?
　　どうなってる？ ・・・・・・・・・・・・・・・・・・・・・ 146
Whatever　どうでもいい ・・・・・・・・・・・・・・ 145
Why don't you do it yourself?
　　かってにやれば？ ・・・・・・・・・・・・・・・・・・・・ 58
Wonderful　すばらしい ・・・・・・・・・・・・・・・ 106
Worries me　きになる ・・・・・・・・・・・・・・・・ 76

Y

You can do it if you try
　　やればできる ・・・・・・・・・・・・・・・・・・・・・・・ 215
You can if you feel interested
　　きがむいたら ・・・・・・・・・・・・・・・・・・・・・・・・ 71
You can say that again　いえてる ・・・・・・ 30
You can't suddenly say that
　　きゅうにいわれてもこまる ・・・・・・・・・・・・・ 82
You don't have to rush
　　あわてなくていい ・・・・・・・・・・・・・・・・・・・・ 23
You don't need to force yourself
　　むりしなくていい ・・・・・・・・・・・・・・・・・・・ 202
You should've told me
　　いってくれればよかったのに ・・・・・・・・・・・ 34
(Your / my) imagination　きのせい ・・・・・ 77
You're cold　つめたいなあ ・・・・・・・・・・・・ 140
You're Irresponsible
　　いいかげんだなあ ・・・・・・・・・・・・・・・・・・・・ 24
You're joking　じょうだんじゃない ・・・・・・ 104
You're nasty　つめたいなあ ・・・・・・・・・・・ 140
You're on a right track
　　いいせんいってる ・・・・・・・・・・・・・・・・・・・・ 26
You're mistaken　ごかいです ・・・・・・・・・・ 89
You're not a child
　　こどもじゃないんだから ・・・・・・・・・・・・・・・ 92
You're on your own, not my problem
　　しらない ・・・・・・・・・・・・・・・・・・・・・・・・・・ 105
You're one to talk　よくいうよ ・・・・・・・・ 218

231

● 監修者

水谷 信子（みずたに のぶこ）
お茶の水女子大学・明海大学名誉教授、元アメリカ・カナダ大学連合日本研究センター教授、元ラジオ講座「100万人の英語」講師など

● 著者

高橋 尚子（たかはし なおこ）　熊本外語専門学校専任講師
松本 知恵（まつもと ちえ）　　NSA日本語学校専任講師
黒岩しづ可（くろいわ しづか）　元日本学生支援機構非常勤講師

レイアウト	オッコの木スタジオ／ポイントライン
DTP	オッコの木スタジオ
カバーデザイン	花本浩一
翻訳	Alex Ko Ransom ／ Susan Mast ／ Shin Hattori ／ Michiyo Miyake

すぐに使える 日本語会話 超ミニフレーズ 発展210

平成28年（2016年）　2月10日　初版第1刷発行
平成29年（2017年）　10月10日　　　第2刷発行

著　者	高橋尚子／松本知恵／黒岩しづ可
発行人	福田富与
発行所	有限会社Jリサーチ出版
	〒166-0002　東京都杉並区高円寺北2-29-14-705
電　話	03(6808)8801（代）　FAX 03(5364)5310
編集部	03(6808)8806
	http://www.jresearch.co.jp
印刷所	株式会社シナノ パブリッシング プレス

ISBN 978-4-86392-263-1
禁無断転載。なお、乱丁、落丁はお取り替えいたします。

©2016　Naoko Takahashi, Chie Matsumoto, Shizuka Kuroiwa All rights reserved.
Printed in Japan